Rivers of the Heart
A Fly-Fishing Memoir

BOOKS BY
STEVE RAYMOND

Kamloops: An Angler's Study of the Kamloops Trout

The Year of the Angler

The Year of the Trout

Backcasts: A History of the Washington Fly Fishing Club, 1939–1989

Steelhead Country

The Estuary Flyfisher

Rivers of the Heart

Rivers of the Heart
A Fly-Fishing Memoir

Steve Raymond

Illustrated by August C. Kristoferson

Skyhorse Publishing

In memory of

LEW and ELIZABETH BELL

CONTENTS

ACKNOWLEDGMENTS

Many people contributed to this book in ways both large and small. I especially wish to thank the following:

August C. "Kris" Kristoferson, my friend and fellow angler, whose fine illustrations grace these pages.

Colonel Cliff Jefferies and his wife, Maureen, my generous hosts on the River Dee, and Frank Webster, our mutual friend, who put us in touch with one another.

Bill and Loraine Jollymore for their kindness and friendship and their appreciation of history. Fly-fishing historians should be grateful that fate entrusted the long-lost legacy of Bill Nation to Bill Jollymore's thoughtful care, and I'm glad our common interest in Nation's work has made us friends.

Tommy Gay, my gracious host at Turneffe Island Lodge.

Howard Rossbach, who introduced me to the wonderful salmon fishing on the Miramichi.

Roberta Smith of the Seattle Opera Association for putting me in touch with Nicolai Ohotnikov and Vladimir Chernov (in an earlier life Roberta was known as Roberta Poltroon of that zany piscatorial periodical, *The Wretched Mess News*).

And last but certainly not least, Nick Lyons for his confidence and patience.

Blame me, not any of them, for any disagreement with the opinions or conclusions expressed in these pages.

— STEVE RAYMOND

PREFACE

$\mathbb{A}$ river is always in a hurry. Glints of light and color flash from the planes and angles of its restless current, distorted visual echoes of the surrounding earth and sky. Sometimes its mirrorlike surface darkens momentarily to reveal a glimpse of mysteries hidden in the river's depths, then just as quickly conceals them once again. The sound of a river is equally mysterious, a soft rush of intermingled hollow notes, chaotic and yet somehow rhythmically compelling, an endless symphony of dashing water.

My memory is like a river, reflecting glints and mysteries from the past. The sight or sound of a river, any river, reminds me of all the other rivers I have seen or heard or fished, of the things that

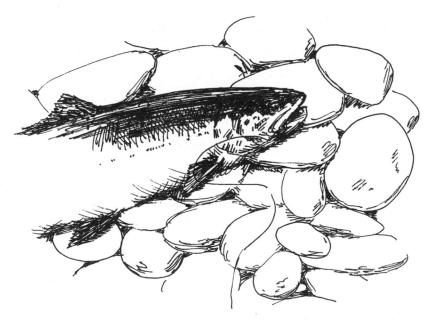

happened in or around them, of the people, places, and events that help define each river in my mind. In the curious way that the mind works, one memory sometimes leads to another, triggering recollections of other waters—lakes, estuaries, or the tropical flats of distant seas. Most of these remembrances are pleasant, as fishing memories ought to be; some are provocative, a few even dimly painful. None are indifferent.

They begin in the headwaters of my life. It was my great good fortune to have both a father and a mother who fished and who saw to it that I began fishing at a very early age. Thanks to them I can now look back on more than a half century of angling experience, more than most people are allotted, and yet still dare hope for many years more.

In the passage of so many years an angler learns that the acts of fishing, and catching fish, are only part of what draws him to the water; he begins to understand that what matters as much, or even more, are the people he meets, the places he visits, the things he observes, uses, or collects, the lessons he learns, and the thoughts, ideas, and fantasies that grow from all these experiences. Some of these demand to be shared.

Hence this book—the memoir of a lifetime of rivers and other waters, and of the people, places, things, realities, and fantasies that define them. These are my rivers of the heart.

— STEVE RAYMOND

PART I

People

CHAPTER ONE

A Few Good Men

Fly fishing is a solitary sport but the enjoyment of it is not. This is one of the great paradoxes of the sport. Each angler must face the fish alone, depending only upon his individual skill or luck, and nothing ever can or should interfere with that sacred and intensely personal one-on-one relationship. But the enjoyment of fly fishing somehow is always magnified or enhanced when another person is along to witness what happens, or simply to talk about it before and afterward. Usually that person is a fishing partner.

There are, of course, many more practical and pragmatic reasons for having a fishing partner. The task of planning a trip is easier when divided between two people, and sharing the costs and the driving makes equal sense. Two sets of hands are always better than one when it's time to set up camp or do the chores, and there is always an added measure of safety in having someone else along. But the need for an understanding friend—someone who can share the joy of angling triumphs and help shoulder the burden of inevitable disappointments, someone who speaks the language of the sport and is able to express the same things that you see and think and feel— that, I believe, is always truly at the heart of the matter.

Choosing a fishing partner is something like choosing a lover. Compatibility must be established at the very start, for the two of you will be spending many hours together in close-quarter venues such as pickup trucks, small airplanes, drift boats, leaky tents, and neon-lit diners. Thus it is essential that you have similar tastes in important matters like food, drink, music, and humor—especially humor. It is also important that you should be roughly equal in fishing ability and experience so that one of you is not more consistently successful than the other, which might breed resentment.

I have been fortunate to have a number of loyal and understanding fishing partners in my life. Since I come from a fishing family, it's hardly surprising that some have been family members—mainly my father, mother, wife, and son—but there have been many others who were not related. They include some of the closest friends I've ever had.

One of the first, when I was still a young man, was Ward McClure. We were close in age but vastly different in background; I had grown up mostly in the Northwest, while he had been raised in the hill country of western North Carolina, a fact evident from his speech. He spoke with a thick, slowly articulated "you-all" accent, which he sometimes exaggerated purposely to disarm city folks, making them think they were dealing with some sort of country bumpkin. This they did at their peril, for Ward's down-home rustic manner concealed a razor-sharp mind—he had advanced degrees in electrical engineering and business administration—and a well-honed sense of humor.

As a youngster Ward had fished for brook trout in the small streams of the North Carolina hills, and when he came to Seattle he adapted this angling experience to the much larger rivers of the Pacific Northwest. He married a girl who had been a friend of my wife's since childhood, and that was how we met; as couples we socialized often, and when Ward and I discovered a common passion for fly fishing we began going fishing together as often as we could.

We also both tied our own flies, and these efforts were greatly abetted by another skill Ward imported from his North Carolina childhood—running traplines for small game. He set traps around the edges of Seattle's suburbs and harvested a steady supply of small furry pelts that provided us with materials for dubbing and hair wings.

Cooking was another of his talents; he had earned money for college working as a chef in a Mexican restaurant, and an uncle in New Mexico occasionally sent him nuclear-hot chilies. These Ward used to prepare the tastiest enchiladas I have ever eaten: great, succulent mounds of meat, tomatoes, lettuce, onions, and cheese, topped with a fried egg. They were also by far the hottest enchiladas I have ever eaten; the first bite would clear your sinuses for a week, and the last one would leave you feeling as if your brain had been laundered. When we were fishing, I gladly deferred the cooking chores to Ward; my culinary talents, such as they are, always have tended more toward consumption than production anyway.

Mostly we fished small streams in the Cascade foothills or some of the many scattered lowland lakes and beaver ponds in the Puget Sound Basin, but we also often enjoyed fishing a small alpine lake in the South Cascades. We were camped there on that historic day in July 1969 when the radio told us the spacecraft *Eagle* had made the first landing on the surface of the moon. We caught and released dozens of brook trout that afternoon, then raced home just in time to turn on the television and watch Neil Armstrong take his giant step for mankind.

On another less historic occasion we fished a lowland lake with a large population of lizardlike aquatic newts—more newts than trout, or at least so it seemed on the day we were there. Ward caught one of the newts and decided to take it home for a pet. He put it in a bucket of water, which he kept on the outside balcony of the upstairs apartment where he lived with his wife, Chris. Occasionally he threw some garden dirt into the bucket; the dirt apparently contained something that provided nourishment for the newt, which grew to astonishing size, although just how Ward knew a newt could subsist on dirt was something I never learned.

One frigid winter night we visited the apartment and I inquired how the newt was getting along in the cold weather.

"Oh mah gawd, Ah forgot ahll about it," Ward said. "Ah'll bet the po' thang's froze stiff."

We went out onto the balcony and looked in the bucket; sure enough, there was a thick layer of ice on top. Ward found an ice pick and chipped away until he broke through and found the newt, which was as stiff as a freshly starched shirt. All efforts to revive it failed, leaving us with the problem of what to do with a dead newt. Ward considered for a moment, then took it inside the apartment and put it in the garbage disposal; there the newt met its unfortunate demise in a series of ugly grinding sounds while Chris shrieked in the background.

Another time, after we had spent a day fishing for beaver-pond trout in the tangled Oak Patch country near Bremerton, I was at the wheel of the truck as we raced toward the ferry landing in the hope of catching one of the evening's last boats back to Seattle. We had just started down a long slope through a thick, dark patch of woods when a pair of stray cats bolted from the trees and dashed in front of the truck; I had no time to react and the truck hit one of them squarely, killing it on the spot.

Dismayed, I glanced over at Ward. Staring straight ahead, with a deadpan expression on his face, he said: "How cum yew missed t'othah one?"

That was an example of Ward's sense of humor at its best—or perhaps its worst. We shared many good times together, laughed a lot, and caught many fish before his career took him away first to

Texas, then later all the way to Singapore. I wonder what he catches in his trapline over there?

I have written elsewhere of Alan Pratt, another of my fishing partners, but there will always be more to tell. Tall, lanky, sparse of hair, gentle of disposition, and keen of wit, Al made his living as a cartoonist for *The Seattle Times*, where I also worked. We made many memorable trips together, seeking trout in the rivers of Yellowstone and steelhead in the Deschutes and Stillaguamish, more trout in the lakes of the Columbia Basin, and most often sea-run cutthroat and Pacific salmon in the estuaries of Puget Sound and Hood Canal.

Al was as much an artist working with wood as he was with a cartoonist's pen, and he designed and built a wooden pram especially for use in the estuaries. To propel the craft he chose a clanky old outboard motor with just a little too much horsepower, and sometimes, when he forgot and cranked the motor up to full throttle, it would push the pram's bow under water; then boat, motor, and Al would all plunge quickly to the bottom. Al's other fishing companions and I rescued him from such misadventures so many times it became something of a joke.

Then the state decreed that all boats with outboard motors had to be registered. Owners were required to report their boat's model name and hull number; if the boat had no name or number, then the state would assign them. Since Al had built his own pram it lacked both model name and hull number, but he was not the sort who would allow some faceless state bureaucrat to decide such important matters. Instead, he made up a name and number of his own, engraved them on a metal plate, and bolted it to the pram's transom. Then he copied them onto a registration form and sent it to the state licensing agency. One can only imagine the reaction of the agent who issued the registration for the boat called *Sinkmaster No. 1.*

At one point in our friendship, when I was seriously considering a job offer from another newspaper, Al decided a gift would be in order for what he thought was my impending departure. He purchased a bottle of fine bourbon, removed the manufacturer's label, and replaced it with a hand-lettered label of his own. It read:

STEVE RAYMOND'S OLD EDITOR STRAIGHT SOUR MASH WHISKEY

Distilled from only the finest aged corn and dribbled slowly down through aged vats of charcoal, hun feathers and moose dung, aged in herring casks for nigh onto four days, and bottled in jugs.

Guaranteed to cure chilblains, acne, shyness, psoriasis, stammering, wind knots, typographical errors, Indian uprisings and some venereal infections.

The surgeon general claims that this stuff is hazardous to health, but what the hell does he know?

In the end I turned down the job, but Al gave me the bottle anyway and we ended up splitting the contents. Now empty but still bearing its one-of-a-kind label, the bottle sits on a shelf in my office, an enduring relic of our friendship—and of Al's irrepressible sense of humor.

Al and I fished together more than 25 years, even after he retired from *The Times* and moved to an island north of Seattle. He brightened many campfires with wonderful stories told in a slow, droll way with his magnificently rich vocabulary, and he always seemed to have exactly the right words for any occasion. In the fall of

1993 he and his wife, Wilma, left for an extended trip to the Southwest, a trip I followed vicariously through his letters, always full of descriptive detail and wry humor. Increasingly his letters also betrayed impatience to return home to the Northwest so we could resume our search for bright sea-run cutthroat in the fog-shrouded estuaries we both loved. And then came the telephone call with the shocking news that Al had died suddenly in Arizona.

No man ever had a better friend than he was, and although I still often fish in the estuaries, it's never quite the same without Al nearby, casting from his precarious pram, always ready with an ingenuous remark to suit the occasion.

Any angler would have been proud to have Enos Bradner as a fishing partner. Brad was in his seventies when I met him but still an impressive physical specimen, lean and spare with ramrod posture and hair as white as the plumage of the snow geese he sometimes hunted. His eyes, deep set under a wrinkled brow, were the color of rivers under sunlight, and when he smiled the many furrows in his weathered face would deepen so it looked as if he were smiling in several places at once. He could be gracious, kind, and incredibly charming; he could also be forceful, intimidating, and incredibly stubborn. Among Northwest anglers he was a legend in his own time, and though we were nearly half a century apart in age, we became the very closest of friends.

We met in 1965, a few months after I went to work for *The Times* as a cub reporter. Brad was the newspaper's outdoor editor, a job it seemed he'd held forever, and his thrice-weekly column, "The Inside on the Outdoors," was said to be the most widely read newspaper feature in the state. The artist's portrait of Bradner that appeared with each column had made his face recognizable throughout the Northwest, and his fame as an expert fly fisher was unsurpassed. He had been charter president of the Washington Fly Fishing Club, a founding officer of the Federation of Fly Fishers, and author of a pioneering book, *Northwest Angling,* and to me he seemed almost godlike, a larger-than-life figure. When I finally mustered the courage to invite him fishing, I was surprised at his ready acceptance. We hit it off immediately on that first trip and began fishing together often.

I soon discovered there were some real advantages in associating with Bradner. One was that I nearly always learned something when we fished together, either just by watching him or by listening to his endless stories. Another was that his well-known name and face gave him entry to places that were off limits to most anglers. Owners of private waters seemed only too eager to have the famous Enos Bradner sample their fishing, and of course his young friend—What was your name again?—was always welcome to come along.

Wherever we traveled, Brad would point out his favorite places to eat or stay, and it wasn't long before I knew them all by heart. His idea of a good motel was one that would allow dogs or maybe even horses; his notion of a fine restaurant was one that served fried chicken, which was about the toughest thing his dentures could handle. My fishing diary is filled with accounts of scores of trips with Brad, but one in particular always makes me smile—although it didn't seem very funny at the time.

We had planned a spring trout-fishing foray to the Columbia Basin and on the morning of departure I called for Brad at his apartment on Seattle's Capitol Hill. He lived upstairs in an old L-shaped brick building with a center courtyard bordered by surface-level garages. Another apartment building stood on a third side of the courtyard, and a brick wall bounded the fourth. I parked my truck in the courtyard and waited for Brad to back his little station wagon out of one of the garages so we could retrieve his boat, which he kept on a wooden frame suspended by ropes from the garage ceiling. After we finished loading the boat on top of my truck and the station wagon was back in his garage, we started on our way.

It turned out to be one of those trips where nearly everything goes wrong. Our first stop was at Nunnally Lake, home of big rainbow trout and then accessible by a gravel road that crossed a set of railroad tracks. The crossing was ungraded, so it had to be negotiated carefully, but we cleared that obstacle without difficulty and drove on to the lake. When we got there the wind was blowing—not just a gentle breeze, but a screaming gale, the likes of which Columbia Basin anglers know all too well. We sat in the truck and waited for the wind to subside, staring in silence for an hour or more at the ragged rows of whitecaps marching down the lake while the truck shuddered in the gusts. When the wind showed no signs of dying down, we decided to drive to Dry Falls Lake instead.

On the way out, I tried to ease the truck over the high rails of the ungraded railroad crossing, but it came down with a hard shock that cracked the exhaust manifold. The engine's racket instantly filled the cab, so loud we had to shout to make ourselves heard.

I wasn't happy about the cracked manifold but there was nothing I could do about it immediately, so we drove on noisily to Dry Falls. The wind was blowing there, too, but the steep cliffs around the lake offered a little protection, so we unloaded our boats and tried to fish. The wind grew steadily stronger and after an hour Brad gave up and took refuge in the truck. I kept on fishing, trying to time my casts between the explosive, howling gusts, but it was no use, and finally I gave up, too. We loaded up the boats, held a brief council of war, and decided to head for Vantage, a little town on the Columbia River. There we would spend the night and hope for better conditions in the morning. Vantage isn't much of a place, but from previous trips with Brad I knew it had a restaurant that served fried chicken and a single motel that probably would have been delighted to admit dogs, horses, or even the entire cargo of Noah's Ark.

It was early evening when we drove into Vantage, tired and cranky from fighting the wind and shouting over the unmuffled sound of the truck's engine. We pulled up at the motel and stared incredulously at a sign that said NO VACANCY. The motel was indeed full, probably for the first time in its history. There wasn't another within 30 miles.

My frustration reached its limits. "To hell with this," I told Brad. "We're going home." He didn't object, probably because he wasn't having much fun either.

The long drive westward over Snoqualmie Pass took several hours and it was nearly 1 A.M. when I turned into the darkened courtyard of Brad's apartment. The truck, with its broken manifold, made a tremendous racket—THRUMBLETHRUMBLETHRUM-BLE—that echoed off the brick walls of the courtyard and the adjoining building and reverberated through the neighborhood.

When I stopped, Brad got out of the truck and slammed the door. Several floors up a light went on, followed quickly by another.

"I'll have to back out the station wagon so we can put the boat away," Brad shouted over the THRUMBLE of the truck's engine. Another upstairs light went on.

Brad fumbled for his keys, found the right one, and unlocked the garage door. It had been a long time since the hinges were oiled, if they ever had been, and the door went up with a loud, metallic screech. More lights came on, and I could see head-and-shoulder silhouettes framed in several windows. "Hurry up before we get killed," I shouted to Brad, expecting a shower of flowerpots at any moment.

Brad got into the station wagon and started it. On an earlier hunting trip he'd gotten stuck in a sandbank and damaged the muffler, which he hadn't bothered to have fixed. The station wagon started with a high-pitched URDLEURDLEURDLEURDLE, a sort of tenor counterpoint to the bass THRUMBLETHRUMBLE-THRUMBLE of my truck. Brad put the station wagon in gear and it stalled, so he started it again.

By this time most of the lights in the apartment house were on and I could hear angry shouts from the upper floors while I tried furiously to untie the knots that held Brad's boat on top of my truck. He backed the station wagon out of the garage and left the motor running, URDLEURDLEURDLEURDLE. We got the boat off my truck, carried it into the garage, and lifted it into its frame. Brad drove the station wagon back into the garage and closed the door with another metallic screech and a loud slam.

Now every upstairs light was on and it was as bright as day in the courtyard. The angry shouts of tenants threatened to drown out the noise of my truck, but I waited until Brad was safely inside before I headed for the driveway. Something hard bounced off the cab of my truck, but I scarcely heard it over the THRUMBLETHRUM-BLETHRUMBLE.

The next day I had the manifold replaced and the truck ran quietly again. But it was a long time before I had the courage to drive it around Brad's apartment house again.

Brad and I fished for steelhead, shad, landlocked salmon, and trout in public and private waters all over the Northwest. He became almost a second father to me, and he was "Uncle Enos" to my children, who loved to sit in his lap while he read them stories. He lived into his 92nd year, one of the great friends of my life, a lifelong bachelor and the most fiercely independent man I ever knew.

Ed Foss was another good friend and frequent fishing partner. I met him when I joined the Washington Fly Fishing Club, where he was the consummate volunteer; if the club had any job that needed doing, Ed was always the first to step forward and offer his services. Warm, generous, likable, and possessing a fine sense of humor, he was the ideal fishing companion.

A native of Bend, Oregon, Ed had been a promising baseball prospect who had just signed a major-league contract when he was drafted to fight in World War II. The war sidetracked any dreams of baseball glory, and by the time I met him he was middle aged and working as office manager at a firm that manufactured industrial gases. He was fond of telling the story of an office picnic where someone had the idea of using a barrel of liquid nitrogen to chill the beer and soda pop. Naturally the beer and pop cans froze in the super-cold nitrogen, then ruptured, and after a while their combined contents began oozing out in a rainbow-colored semiliquid blob like something from a science-fiction movie.

Frozen substances figured in more than one Ed Foss story. He enjoyed fishing Sparks Lake, high in the Oregon Cascades near Bend, where he liked to camp next to an old lava flow. The lava had deep crevices full of ice that probably had been there since the lava cooled a couple of thousand years earlier, and Ed liked to chip off some of the ice for cocktails. He always said 12-year-old bourbon tasted better with 2,000-year-old ice.

To Ed I owe some of the best fishing I've ever had. He steered me to my first estuary cutthroat and persuaded me to try the then-fabulous dry-fly fishing for transplanted Atlantic salmon in Oregon's Hosmer Lake. Along with our passion for fly fishing we also shared an appreciation for classical music, and on one trip to Hosmer Lake Ed took along a battery-powered portable stereo set. He set up the speakers on either side of the campfire, and one evening while we were relaxing and listening to music, a dog came trotting into camp and wandered over to one of the speakers. Apparently thinking it resembled a fire hydrant, the dog did what dogs always do to fire hydrants; there was a sudden blue flash, a large puff of smoke, and that was the last classical music we heard on that trip.

Tanwax Lake near Tacoma was another of Ed's favorites. Fall evenings on the lake usually brought forth a hatch of large, blood-red chironomids that Ed imitated with a fly he called the Pink Lady, quite different from the traditional pattern of that name. Sometimes I joined him and we would catch heavy rainbows on his Pink Ladies until it was too dark to fish any longer.

Tanwax Lake also held black crappie, which rose as willingly as the trout, and it was impossible to keep from catching one now and then. Ed was contemptuous of these non-native, dinner-plate-shaped fish; he called them "Frisbees," and whenever he caught one he would remove the hook and see how far he could sail the fish across the lake. He achieved some pretty fair distances, too.

It was a measure of the affection and respect in which Ed was held by his fellow anglers that so many gathered for a floating wake on Tanwax Lake after his sudden death from a heart attack. It was an impressive sight: A flotilla of small boats filled with Ed's angling friends converged at twilight in a little bay he loved to fish. The boats were formed into a circle and all hands raised glasses in a final toast to their old friend while Ed's ashes were committed to the deep. A weighted Pink Lady was dropped in after them. Ed would have liked that.

I've been blessed with other good fishing companions. Errol Champion and I sampled many waters together before his work took him to Juneau, Alaska, where I'm certain he has better fishing than he could now find around Seattle. Lew Bell was a great friend whose cabin was near mine on the North Fork of the Stillaguamish; we spent many pleasant hours together fishing the river or swapping tales around campfires. Ralph Wahl taught me more about steelhead fishing than I learned from anyone else, and entrusted me with the secrets of some of his most treasured places. I met Dave Draheim at Hosmer Lake many years ago and now we fish there together every year, and sometimes travel to other angling destinations in the Northwest or beyond. And there are scores of others with whom I've fished once or a few times—perhaps not yet enough to consider them full-fledged fishing partners, but who's to say we won't fish together more often in the future?

Anglers must always face the fish alone, and that is how it should be. But the very best fishing moments will ever be those we spend in the company of a partner and a friend.

CHAPTER TWO

Rediscovering Bill Nation

Bill Nation was one of those fortunate people who lived in the right place at the right time. The place was British Columbia and the time was the 1930s, when the rich lakes of the Kamloops region, most having recently been stocked for the first time, were coming on line with trout of incredible size. They offered spectacular fly fishing of a kind never since equaled, and Nation was a legendary guide and fly tier whose patterns became the favorites of several generations of Kamloops trout anglers.

Nation was described by his friend, writer Roderick Haig-Brown, as "a small, slender, soft-voiced man who talks a great deal but listens well enough to seem almost silent." Another writer, Bruce Hutchison, declared that Nation "knew trout better than any other British Columbian."

"Careless of fame or money, he would row you around Paul Lake, his favorite, or any other lake you fancied for a few dollars a day," Hutchison wrote in *The Fraser*, a history of the Fraser River country. "After an hour's fishing with him the richest American tycoon was subdued and humble in this shy man's presence. Beside his life of innocence and content, the perfect companionship of man and nature, your own life suddenly appeared for the failure it was."

Hutchison was right in describing Nation's life as one most anglers would envy, also right when he said Nation was careless about money. When Nation died in November 1940 he was virtually penniless and the managers of Echo Lodge at Paul Lake, Nation's headquarters, were forced to sell his tackle to pay burial expenses.

With that, nearly all visible evidence of Nation's life disappeared, leaving little for future angling historians to examine—just a few old photographs and a small framed display of flies on the wall of Echo Lodge. Now even the lodge itself is gone, and along with it the last tangible evidence of the life and times of Bill Nation.

Or at least that's what everyone thought.

Then, in 1995, 55 years after Nation's death, a remarkable discovery came to light—an old trunk bearing a treasure of artifacts from his life. Here at last was evidence of his work, a wealth of material angling historians could grasp and examine and perhaps use to glean something of the substance of the man who contributed so much to the lore and legend of Northwest angling.

Arthur William Nation was born June 29, 1881, in Bristol, England. He was trained as a pharmacist and worked briefly at the trade, though little else is known of his early life, or where or how he learned to fish, but when he arrived in British Columbia sometime in the 1920s his fly-fishing and fly-tying skills were already fully developed. Photographs show him as a small, lean man with large, angular features, usually wearing horn-rimmed glasses and often dressed in a bulky, high-collared sweater.

His first guiding experience in British Columbia was on the Little River, where big Kamloops trout gathered to feed on loose sockeye salmon spawn in the fall and returned in the spring to feast on emerging sockeye alevins. Nation later moved to Paul Lake, a rich, clear lake in a side valley off the North Thompson River, not far from Kamloops. Like many lakes in the region, Paul had abundant weed-covered shoals teeming with scuds and insects, which provided ample food for foraging trout. It was an ideal spot for fly fishing and also an unusually scenic lake, sprawling across the bottom of a verdant valley between steep, pine-clad slopes.

Nation made his headquarters at Echo Lodge at the west end of the lake. The lodge had been accessible by road for only a few years and still lacked such amenities as electricity or telephone service when he moved there, but it was nevertheless considered a first-class place by the standards of the day.

Paul Lake had received its first trout in 1908, and by the time Nation got there these fish had long since passed their initial spurt of growth and the lake had settled down to yield steady catches of trout averaging 2 to 3 pounds, with some larger. Nation guided on Paul and other lakes nearby, such as Pinantan, Knouff, Devick's Beaver, Peterhope, and Hihium, where the trout sometimes were very much larger. He also began experimenting with the fly patterns that were soon to become famous, working by day when there were no clients to guide, or straining his eyes at night to tie by the uncertain light of coal-oil lamps.

Nation was thoroughly grounded in the traditions of classic British salmon and sea-trout flies and his Kamloops trout patterns clearly reflect the influence of those traditions, but they also reveal a sound knowledge of the insect life of the Kamloops trout lakes. He was not a strict imitationist, apparently believing instead that a fly pattern should merely suggest the appearance of a natural insect, or create an impression of it. Neither was he precise in his work; his flies lack the neat, well-proportioned, carefully trimmed look popular among contemporary tiers, tending instead to have soft outlines and ragged silhouettes. This was partly by design—Nation wanted his flies to have a soft "buggy" look—and partly probably due to the relatively unsophisticated tools and techniques available to him at the time, or the primitive conditions under which he worked (having tried tying flies by the light of a coal-oil lamp, I know how difficult it can be).

For materials, Nation used what he could obtain locally, importing others from the British firms of Hardy Bros., Allcock, and Veniard's. He liked flash in his flies, which he usually achieved with a silver tag or rib, and he favored large hooks with a Limerick bend. But it was his strikingly original choice of materials and the ways he blended them that truly set his flies apart.

His Gray and Green Nymph patterns are good examples. Intended to suggest the appearance of dragonfly nymphs, these were undoubtedly Nation's two most ungainly (some might say ugly) patterns, but they reveal an especially ingenious combination of materials. Nation began each pattern by building up a fat underbody of gray or green wool or chenille, then wrapped it completely with gray mallard breast feathers, which were bound on with tinsel or thread. The result was a fat, bulky fly, similar in shape to the natural. When it was wet the color of the underbody would show through the mottled feathers of the mallard breast, creating a deadly realistic effect. These patterns probably were the closest to "exact" imitations that Nation ever made.

Another example of his originality was his practice of carrying a bottle of peroxide so he could bleach the dyed-green seal fur bodies of his Sedge patterns to match exactly the color of the insects hatching at the time.

He advertised his flies as "guaranteed to kill" and sold them for $2.50 a dozen—top dollar in the 1930s. His most famous patterns were Nation's Black, Nation's Red, Nation's Blue, Nation's Fancy, his Green Sedge, Silver and Mallard, Silvertip, and Silvertip Sedge, Nation's Special, and his Gray and Green Nymphs.

In a 1934 advertisement Nation promised "at least 100 trout a week" for clients during a season extending from April 16 to November 30. His fee was $35 a week. "Each season I net for clients up to 70 trout a day in number, and of larger fish, up to 60 lbs. weight of trout a day, all on the fly," the advertisement said.

As Nation's reputation grew he began to receive more clients than he could handle, so he sometimes employed other guides to help; two who worked with him regularly were Alex Vinnie and John Richmond "Jack" Morrill, the latter a nephew of V. A. Scott, proprietor of Echo Lodge. Nation also became friends with Charles Mottley, a government fisheries biologist who chose Paul Lake as the site for the first serious study of the life history of the Kamloops trout, and with Haig-Brown, then a young writer researching his first book on North American fishing. Aware of Nation's reputation as an angler and fly tier, Haig-Brown studied his fly patterns and the theories behind them, and in his two-volume work, *The Western Angler,* published in 1939, he said this:

> There is no better Kamloops fisherman than Nation, and he may well claim credit for many of the traditions and methods that already belong to the sport of fly fishing for Kamloops trout; he is a boldly constructive fisherman and full of theories. Since he is well read in the literature of angling, widely experienced in the fishing of at least two or three countries, and has been able to add to this experience and knowledge much of the scientific information offered by Mottley and the other good men who have worked at Paul Lake, even his seemingly wildest theories are likely to be built on fairly solid ground. But for all that he is wholly fisherman, not scientist, and his ideas are likely to have in them more of poetry than of treatise.

Haig-Brown noted that "at least at the present stage of angling development" (meaning the 1930s), wet flies were more important than dry flies in the Kamloops trout lakes, "and it seems altogether probable that more fish are caught on 'fancy' flies than on those which attempt to imitate natural insects." He included six of Nation's patterns on a list of such "fancy" flies, noting that all had silver tinsel on the rear third of their bodies, giving them the dash of flash that Nation favored.

Haig-Brown also studied the contents of the "Paul Lake Honour Book," a record of notable catches from 1921 through 1936. The book listed 119 fly-caught trout weighing from 3-$\frac{1}{2}$ to 7-$\frac{3}{4}$ pounds; of those, 46 had been caught on a Nation's Special. Haig-Brown remarked on "the amazing success" of this fly, noting it was responsible for nearly 40 percent of the fish recorded in the book.

Haig-Brown also quoted letters from Nation, including one in which the famous guide explained the reasoning behind his Dragonfly Nymphs:

> Tying the dragon nymphs as I go, I find that the col-oring should vary with the quality of the light. If heavily overcast, use a light mottled gray; in bright sunlight use a dull green. The [Nation's] Special and the Gray and Green Dragon Nymphs account for the bulk of the larger Kamloops. The largest on fly in recent years weighed 17 lbs. and took a No. 4 Gray Nymph. The two largest last summer went 8-$\frac{1}{4}$ each, and both took a No. 4 Gray Nymph. . . .

> On August 14th of 1936 I found the trout at Surrey Lake on the feed and took over 100 lbs. weight with the one rod before lunch, using No. 4 Special; two best 12 lbs. each. Would not have kept any fish at all, but found a rancher's haying outfit had the only boat and they agreed to let me have it on condition that they could have any fish I caught.

In a later revised edition of *The Western Angler,* published after Nation's death, Haig-Brown said Nation "set great store by the motion of the wet fly at all times, and I am sure he was quite right. 'Underwater life movements,' he once wrote me, 'might be classified into those that flick like a prawn, the large dragon nymphs; those that crawl like a snake on a boardwalk, in one plane, as the *Enallagma* (damselfly) nymphs; those that walk like a sheep, as many of the sedge nymphs. And the working of the fly that imitates these forms should also imitate the action of the particular nymph.'"

Nation's innovations went beyond his fly patterns. He tried to transplant the famous "traveling sedge" from nearby Knouff Lake to Paul Lake, whose own sedge hatches were of a different character. This failed, but he did succeed in persuading fisheries managers to introduce crayfish to Paul Lake, thus providing an additional source of food for its trout. And he was at least a half century ahead of his time in suggesting that Kamloops trout should be sterilized so their growth would not be inhibited by sexual maturity. Nobody was listening in the 1930s, but sterilization experiments with Kamloops trout are common now.

The late Seattle outdoor photographer Lee Richardson had a chance encounter with Nation at Devick's Beaver Lake in the spring of 1940, which he later described in his book, *Lee Richardson's B.C.* Richardson and his party had just arrived at the lake and were getting settled when they heard horses approach.

> Going out to investigate I discovered to my immeasurable delight it was the notable guide Bill Nation, with a couple from Bremerton. They had been assigned the newer of the two cabins by the lake, and since they had only one bed and it had started to rain I suggested Bill stay with us, an offer which, after a considerable show of reluctance, he accepted.

This was my only meeting with the unusual man from Paul Lake whose name was already synonymous with the Kamloops country and whose fly patterns will endure so long as there are trout and men worthy of angling for them. At least two of his originals, Nation's Special and Nation's Silvertip, have accompanied me on all subsequent trips—yielding more than usual success, I might say.

This formidable man was shy and soft-spoken, with the manner and appearance of a schoolmaster; and the two nights he spent in our cabin are among the most treasured of my angling memories. . . .

This chance meeting occurred the end of May 1940. Within five months Bill Nation was dead of cancer. If Bill had any premonition the end was so near, no one knew it, because he was not given to talk about such matters.

Nation's last client, in October 1940, was Dr. Bill McMahon of Seattle. Years later he described the ritual Nation went through with his clients:

There was none of the hurly-burly early morning things. You had your breakfast and then he considered the barometer. And it was a very considered judgment on the barometer because it determined where you would fish. And under certain circumstances . . . he would say, "Can't fish today."

I didn't know the formula, but we would go from the high lakes—Peterhope and some of the others—to Paul Lake itself and all the varying stages in between. . . . We always had fine fishing with Bill. He knew he was dying and I think he purposely picked different areas each day, even though the barometer might have said so. He wanted to show us his country and more or less relive his own life. . . .

And, as we learned, we were the last people that he fished with. I left a rod, one of the rods that I had borrowed, so I wrote to Bill after we got home. There was a bit of a delay and then I received a letter from the lady who managed the lodge telling me that Bill had died. She was so sorry, but they had just gathered together all of his tackle and sold it to get some money to take care of his funeral expenses. He didn't have much to show for his lifetime of effort.

Nation's fly patterns remained popular long after his death and others began tying and selling them. That was still true when I wrote about Nation and his flies in my book *Kamloops, an Angler's Study of the Kamloops Trout,* first published in 1971. But angling fashions change, just as they do in other fields, and by the late 1970s fly tiers were becoming preoccupied with "exact" imitations and anglers were becoming more sophisticated in their tastes; Bill Nation's flies gradually began to disappear from the boxes of Kamloops trout anglers, and his legend began disappearing along with them.

That was how matters stood in January 1995 when I received a telephone message from Bill Jollymore. I remembered a man of that name had operated a fly-fishing shop in Kamloops during the 1960s and was known for tying replicas of Nation's patterns. I had even bought flies in his shop once or twice but did not recall ever meeting him face to face, nor had I heard of him since. Yet the name was unusual, so I thought it must be the same man. Why, after so many years, would he be trying to get in touch with me? Especially when we had never even met?

I returned his call and introduced myself. Jollymore explained he had read my book about Kamloops trout, including the parts about Bill Nation and his fly patterns, and that was the reason he had sought me out.

"I've got Bill Nation's fly-tying stuff," he said. "I thought you'd like to see it."

I scarcely believed my ears at first, but Jollymore told a convincing tale. He had indeed been the owner of the fly-fishing shop in Kamloops, which opened in 1964. Initially his business prospered, and before long he found it necessary to take on additional part-time help. The man he hired was Jack Morrill, one of the guides who had worked with Nation at Paul Lake.

The two became friends and Morrill taught Jollymore Nation's tying style. Then one day while Jollymore was visiting Morrill's home, the old guide led him downstairs and pointed to a trunk in the basement. "That's Bill Nation's stuff," he said. Morrill explained that when Nation died he had gathered up his fly-tying materials to keep them from being sold along with his tackle.

But Morrill refused to open the trunk. Later, during subsequent visits, Jollymore said Morrill showed him a few items from the trunk's contents, but would never let him see inside.

Meanwhile, Jollymore's business began to suffer from a long strike in the forest-products industry, lifeblood of the local economy, and eventually he was forced to close the shop in November 1967. After that he left Kamloops and went to Lewiston, Idaho, where he managed a sporting-goods store for ten years, then moved to Washington State. But he never lost contact with his friend Jack Morrill, and never forgot about the mysterious old trunk in Morrill's basement.

In 1994 Morrill died at the age of 79. His widow, Doris, got in touch with Jollymore and asked if he wanted the old trunk. Jollymore

most decidedly did, and went and got it. Now it was at his home near
Olympia. Would I like to see the contents?

I told Jollymore I certainly would, and we made arrangements
to meet. On the appointed day my wife, Joan, and I drove to
Olympia, where we were greeted cordially by Bill and his wife,
Loraine. We got acquainted over a delicious lunch they had prepared, discovering in the course of the conversation that we had
many mutual friends, and then Bill and I climbed a stairway to a
landing where an old steamer trunk sat in the corner. "I can't be sure,
but I think Nation might have brought this with him when he came
over from England," Jollymore said. Judging from the age and
appearance of the trunk, that might well have been the case.

Jollymore opened the trunk and began removing the contents
item by item. He had taken the wise precaution of sealing the fly-
tying materials in protective plastic bags, but otherwise everything
was just as he had found it, he said.

It was like opening a time capsule. Inside the trunk were many
brown paper packets from the British firm of Allcock, all with their
contents and Nation's account number handwritten in black ink on
the outside: "2 doz blue jay hackles for No. 6 Hks; 3 doz Scarlet
Hackles—small; 2 doz dyed swan feathers—blue for No. 2 hooks; 6
doz black hackles for No. 5 Hks; 4 doz white swan feathers for No. 4
Hks and No. 2 Hks"—and so on. Some of the packets had been
opened and their contents partly used, while others were still sealed
with original tape bearing the Allcock logo. The feathers they held
were as bright and firm as they had been on the day they arrived at
Paul Lake so many years before, and I wondered how long it had
taken for them to be shipped all the way from England to the remote
little town of Kamloops, and thought of how eagerly Nation must
have awaited their arrival.

There were also many small glassine envelopes from the famous old English firm of Hardy Bros. Their contents included thrush wings, kingfisher feathers, badger hackle, white yarn, red and orange hackle feathers, moleskin, green-dyed pig's wool, guinea fowl feathers, French partridge, and brown and black hackle feathers.

A small cardboard box held rolls of tinsel, including six rolls of French gold and silver tinsel still packed in their original tissue wrappings. There were many envelopes, some with their flaps sealed, others bound with string—probably by Nation himself— all stuffed with various kinds of fur and feathers, probably of local origin. There was badger fur, green- and yellow-dyed pig's wool, groundhog hair, mallard feathers dyed yellow with picric acid, porcupine quills, grouse wings, and huge quantities of undyed mallard breast feathers. Other materials, not of local origin, included a red ibis skin and several beautifully matched pairs of oak turkey feathers.

Another large packet from Allcock held splendid three-foot lengths of peacock sword, and a newspaper page, dated September 1935, was wrapped around an assortment of teal feathers. Yet another batch of feathers was wrapped in a broadsheet copy of the 1939 British Columbia angling regulations.

An old wooden cigar box disclosed a full cargo of smaller boxes containing many different sizes of hooks, all with a Limerick bend. There were two well-used pieces of fly-tying wax, a worn pair of fly-tying scissors, and a set of hair shears.

Here in our hands were the raw materials and tools that Bill Nation had used to fashion the flies that became part of Northwest fly-fishing history. I could imagine his nimble fingers twisting tinsel on a hook from one of the boxes I held in my hand, dipping into one of those old Hardy glassine envelopes for just the right feather needed next, then using those tarnished old scissors to trim away stray fibers until the fly looked right in Nation's eyes.

Jollymore must have been thinking similar thoughts. "Can't you just imagine the old boy working with this stuff?" he said, handing over another old wooden cigar box.

This box held flies, dozens of them, patterns Nation himself had tied at Echo Lodge so many years ago. There were fine examples of his Green and Gray Nymphs, his famous Green Sedge, Nation's Red, Nation's Special, and Nation's Turkey. Among them were two other famous old British Columbia patterns, a Carey's Special and a Bryan Williams Gray-Bodied Sedge, both tied in their original styles.

The trunk also yielded an old metal fly box containing a large assortment of small British trout flies. Could Nation have brought these flies from England? There was no way to tell, but judging from their age and the selection of patterns—all popular flies in the 1920s—it seemed likely.

There was also a small collection of well-thumbed books, including an undated copy of *Loch Fishing in Theory and Practice,* by R. C. Bridgett, with W. NATION, ECHO LODGE, PAUL LAKE, KAMLOOPS, B.C., handwritten on the flyleaf. A 1922 copy of *Fishing Tackle* by Perry D. Fraser and a 1923 copy of *Practical Fly Fishing* by Larry St. John both had W. NATION inscribed on the front papers. Another 1922 work, *Float & Fly—A Little Book for Anglers,* an anthology edited by Samuel J. Cooker, was signed: [to] WILLIAM NATION—FROM A PUPIL.

Other volumes included a 1917 copy of *Trout Lore* by O. W. Smith, which had been owned by V. A. Scott of Echo Lodge, a 1918 copy of *Wet-Fly Fishing* by E. M. Tod, and a 1919 copy of *Rod & Creel in British Columbia* by Bryan Williams, each with J. R. MORRILL, ECHO LODGE, PAUL LAKE, handwritten on the flyleaf. There was also an old undated angling catalog from C. Farlow & Co., Ltd., London, with pages bound by rivets so they could be replaced by the revisions that Farlow apparently sent out periodically.

Among the envelopes containing fur and feathers were a number bearing Nation's personal letterhead, which included a photograph of the famous guide holding a "17-pound Kamloops rainbow." The return address read: RESEARCH FOUNDATION OF CANADA, WM. NATION, DIRECTOR OF ICHTHYIC GENETICS, PAUL LAKE, KAMLOOPS, B.C. What was this lofty title all about? Haig-Brown's original edition of *The Western Angler* provided the answer, quoting a tongue-in-cheek letter from Nation: "Have appointed myself Director of Ichthyic Genetics in the Research Foundation, having acquired a red-headed stenographer named Jean and am now an authority of the Genes of Heredity."

The trunk also held several old black-and-white photographs of Nation, plus another snapshot that appeared newer than the rest—a stark, simple view of a stone monument with this inscription:

ERECTED IN MEMORY OF BILL NATION OF PAUL LAKE,

KAMLOOPS, BY HIS MANY FISHERMEN FRIENDS AND ADMIRERS.

DIED NOV. 27, 1940.

It seemed likely Morrill had taken the photograph, probably just after the monument was placed on Nation's grave, but Jollymore did not know its location, and neither did I. (British Columbia angling historian Art Lingren later located the grave and monument in a Kamloops cemetery.)

As I sorted through all these marvelous relics, I couldn't help wondering what might become of this historic treasure. Jollymore volunteered the answer, saying he hoped it could be placed on display in a museum. "It's too selfish for one person to own it," he said. By coincidence, I had just agreed to become curator of an exhibition on the history of Northwest fly fishing at the Whatcom Museum of

History and Art in my hometown of Bellingham, Washington. When I told Jollymore this, he quickly offered Nation's materials for the exhibition.

Eighteen months later the exhibition opened with a re-created version of Bill Nation's fly-tying table as one of its main attractions. The table was cluttered with relics from the old trunk—the packages from Allcock and Hardy Bros., boxes of hooks, spools of tinsel, loose feathers, patches of hide, blocks of fly-tying wax, and Nation's tools. A vise held one of the old master's Green Sedge patterns, while other flies were scattered on the table. Nation's books were arranged on a shelf above the table, next to a 1932 calendar, and there were even a few stray feathers strewn on the floor beneath the table—always the trademark of a busy tier. The final touch was provided by a coal-oil lamp next to the vise.

It was hard to look at the display without feeling a kinship with the soft-spoken little guide who had the good luck to live in the right place at the right time and contributed so much to the Northwest angling heritage. Here, after so many years in hiding, was evidence of the man and his work, bringing the shadowy past into bright focus for the first time. Bill Nation had been rediscovered; I hope he never again will be forgotten.

CHAPTER THREE

War and Peace

Sometime long after dark the train crossed the border into East Germany. Through the window of my passenger compartment I strained to see something of the country, but there was only the thick darkness of a late summer night, interrupted at odd intervals by dim clusters of light from distant villages. Finally I gave up looking and tried to doze while the train clicked its monotonous way along the slender web of track extending toward the distant oasis of West Berlin. It was August 1960, and although the summer evening was warm, the chill of the Cold War was at its peak.

Suddenly I was jarred awake by the noisy halting of the train. A glance out the window revealed it was still dark, although I could see a row of bright lights close at hand. The time, according to my wristwatch, was a little past 2 A.M., which meant we were still a long way from Berlin. And this was not a scheduled stop.

I moved to the window, raised it, leaned out to take a look around—and found myself staring into the ugly dark muzzle of a submachine gun. A young soldier dressed in a Soviet Army uniform was holding the weapon, aimed directly at my face. Under the row of lights were other soldiers, all similarly armed, standing in line for as far as I could see in either direction up and down the tracks.

Welcome to East Germany, I thought. Not exactly your typical chamber-of-commerce greeting.

But neither was it surprising. The Soviet forces occupying East Germany had been engaged in one of their periodic campaigns of harassment, arbitrarily cutting off or delaying rail and road access to West Berlin. We had been warned there might be trouble.

When he saw I wasn't about to climb through the window and try to escape, the young soldier lowered his weapon. He glanced around to make sure no officers were in sight, then looked up at me and said something in Russian. He was about 18 years old, with a thatch of blond hair sticking out from under his cap, and like his fellow soldiers he was dressed in a heavy overcoat that must have been desperately uncomfortable in the hot summer night. His manner was not unfriendly—that is, if one could overlook that he had just pointed a submachine gun at my face—but since I spoke no Russian, I had no idea what he had said. I asked if he spoke English, but the young soldier merely shrugged and shook his head. I tried German next, but that only drew another shrug, and I sensed the two of us had just exhausted all our language skills.

Then the Russian pointed at himself and said "Omsk," and I understood he meant that was where he came from. He pointed at me with a questioning look. "Seattle," I said, without much hope. As I expected, he gave no sign he recognized the name. "New York" drew the same response. So did Chicago and Philadelphia.

Suddenly one of the other soldiers gave a quiet whistle; an officer had come into view down the line. The young soldier quickly stepped back in line with his weapon at "port arms" position and stood motionless like his companions. With a sudden jerk, the train started forward, and I watched out the window until the young soldier from Omsk passed out of view beneath the long row of lights in the hot August night.

He was the first Russian I ever met.

It was 30 years before I met any others. As it turned out, they were also uniformed and armed, but their "uniforms" were chest waders, their "arms" were graphite fly rods, and the first thing one of them said to me was: "Do you like beer?"

That's when I knew the Cold War was really over.

The one who asked about the beer was Vladimir Chernov, a young baritone from the Kirov Theater Opera Company in what was then still known as Leningrad, U.S.S.R. We were squeezed tightly into the backseat of a small station wagon heading north from Seattle on Interstate 5. In the front seat were Nicolai Ohotnikov, a veteran bass also from the Kirov Theater, and the driver, Vladimir Gross, a Russian-language instructor at the University of Washington who was acting as our interpreter.

It was late July 1990 and Chernov and Ohotnikov were in Seattle to sing in the Goodwill Arts Festival presentation of Prokofiev's great patriotic Russian opera, *War and Peace,* based on Tolstoy's classic novel. Both were fly fishermen and I had been asked by the Seattle Opera Association to take them fishing. We were headed for my fishing camp on the North Fork of the Stillaguamish River, about 60 miles from Seattle, where I hoped they might have a chance at a summer-run steelhead. Behind us in another car were my wife, Joan, my son, Randy, Chernov's wife, Olga, and Joyce Hersberger, another interpreter.

Most people have a stereotyped image of male opera singers as overweight Italian tenors with egos even larger than their bellies. Nicolai and Vladimir were nothing like that. Each was stocky but neither fat, and Vladimir, the younger of the two, had a smooth, round face and innocent eyes that camouflaged what seemed to be a mischievous personality. Nicolai had the weather-beaten look of long Russian winters and might have passed for a retired prizefighter. Both were vigorous, energetic men who smiled and laughed easily— a couple of regular guys who also just happened to be Russian grand-opera singers and fly fishermen.

Earlier that day they had raided the shelves of one of Seattle's fly-fishing shops, outfitting themselves with brand-new fly rods, waders, vests, reels, lines, spools of leader material, and boxes of flies. Judging from the abundance and quality of their equipment, it looked as if they had made a substantial dent in the U.S. balance-of-payments deficit in a single afternoon.

Nicolai, I had been advised, was an experienced fly fisherman. Vladimir, on the other hand, had fished only once before. The Opera Association had made it clear that I was not to allow either of them to fall in the river, for fear they might catch cold and be unable to sing. That added a little extra challenge to my unfamiliar role as guide.

Vladimir spoke a fair amount of English but Nicolai only a little, so we conversed mostly with the interpreter's help as we drove north. Through the interpreter I learned that Nicolai fished the rivers around Leningrad for grayling, pike, and some kind of trout, although we never were able to find the right words to define exactly what kind of trout he was talking about. He also spoke sadly of the pollution that had taken a severe toll on the fishing near Leningrad, making it necessary to travel ever farther afield in search of good sport—a problem compounded by poor Russian roads and enormous distances.

I was surprised to learn that Nicolai also tied his own flies, despite great difficulty obtaining materials. He told of going into the countryside to bargain with an old woman who had a flock of chickens: He would buy the feathers from her rooster if she promised to dispatch the bird by hitting it over the head instead of cutting its head off, which might damage the precious neck feathers he needed for dry flies. The woman thought he was crazy, but went along with the deal.

Other than the occasional bartered rooster, Nicolai said his only source of plumage was plucking the mediocre hackles from feather dusters. These he used to tie flies during long winters when the rivers were hopelessly frozen but the fishing spirit still burned brightly.

Tying flies at such times "makes me feel closer to the fishing," the interpreter translated. That was a feeling I could well understand.

We turned off the freeway into the valley of the Stillaguamish with its rich bottomland farms and steep timber-clad slopes. Nicolai and Vladimir hailed the scenery with words like "bootiful" and "fantastiche." Our first sight of the river brought forth an excited torrent of Russian from both, and I could see this was indeed a pair of highly enthusiastic fishermen.

When we reached the cabin, I remembered Vladimir's question about beer and fetched a couple of cold ones from the refrigerator. Nicolai downed his in three mighty gulps while Vladimir finished a close second. Both men then rushed to have a look at the river, which prompted another chorus of "bootifuls" and "fantastiches." Then they hurried back to the cabin to put on their new waders and rig up their new rods.

By that time the second car with Randy, Joan, Olga, and Joyce had arrived, and Randy and I also began rigging up. We couldn't keep pace with Nicolai, who soon was out the door and heading for the river. Randy was ready next so I told him to hurry after Nicolai and take him to a quiet spot we called the Pocket, where Vladimir and I would join them as soon as we were ready. The Pocket offered easy wading and I thought it would be a good place to start; I wanted to get some idea of how well Vladimir and Nicolai could navigate in the river before we tried anything more difficult. The North Fork of the Stillaguamish in late summer is usually a gentle river, but it can be very slippery because of algae that grows on the river rocks, and I was mindful of the Opera Association's instructions to be sure these two didn't fall in.

The interpreters had no wading gear so they remained behind, leaving Randy and me on our own to communicate with our Russian guests. I waded out with Vladimir, noting he seemed a little unsteady even in the gentle water of the Pocket, and pointed to the area where he should cast. Having fished with a fly rod only once before, he was anything but a polished caster, but his enthusiasm and strength compensated for what he lacked in skill. He flung the fly line back and forth with alarming cracks like pistol shots, but still managed to get the fly out an impressive distance.

I tried to explain that after each few casts he should take a step or two downstream and cast again, repeating the process until he had methodically covered the whole drift. He nodded that he understood, and seemed to be doing well for an inexperienced fisherman, so after a while I left him and waded downstream to see how Nicolai was getting along.

Nicolai's greater experience was evident in his casting, which was fairly good, and even more so in his wading, which was bold and confident. I pointed out a little wrinkle in the current that marked an underwater boulder, a good resting place for steelhead, and suggested he cast to the spot. He nodded and said "da," so I moved off to get out of his way. When I looked back he had already waded past the spot, avoiding it as carefully as if I had told him it was an alligator's lair. Maybe that's what he thought I said.

Vladimir, meanwhile, was still rooted firmly in the spot where I had left him. And that, it developed, was to be the pattern for our evening of fishing: No matter what Randy and I said or did, Vladimir stayed put, blasting the same water over and over again with brute-strength casts, while Nicolai moved constantly, rarely staying in the same place longer than the time it took to make a single cast. Each time we tried to point out a good holding spot—"fish there," "good place," "cast there"—Nicolai would nod and say "da," then wade around the spot, giving it as wide a berth as he possibly could.

Not surprisingly, neither caught a steelhead. Vladimir, in fact, caught nothing at all, but in one of his rare moves he did manage to slip on a rock and fall in the river. I rushed over to him, fearing the worst, but he quickly regained his feet, wrung the water out of the wet sleeve of his sweater, and resumed fishing as if nothing had happened.

Nicolai, meanwhile, caught and released ten small trout, all probably steelhead smolts. When it became too dark to fish any longer he waded out of the river, grinning broadly, and said "Ten sardines!" But he had also seen one big chinook salmon roll, so at least he knew I was telling the truth when I said the river held much larger fish.

Back at the cabin we demolished a buffet supper that Joan had prepared. We had also invited our riverside neighbor, Bob Headrick, whose springer spaniel delighted the Russians with a trick: Bob told the dog to sit, placed a cracker on her nose, then said "Okay!" and the dog flipped the cracker into the air and caught it in her mouth. Vladimir was so taken with the trick that he decided to try it himself, balancing a cracker on his nose, then flipping it into the air and trying to catch it in his mouth, while everyone laughed.

We talked and joked late into the evening and it was nearly midnight when we dropped the Russians off at the Seattle apartment house where they were staying. Vladimir grinned and shook hands, Olga hugged everybody and planted a big wet kiss on my cheek, and Nicolai pumped my hand vigorously and said "Tank you ferry much. I am ferry hoppy." I was very happy, too, and wished I knew the Russian words to tell them how much I had enjoyed the day.

A few nights later Joan and I attended a performance of *War and Peace*. Nicolai was suitably dignified and grave in his role of Field Marshal Kutuzov and Vladimir made a grand entrance as Prince Andrei, resplendent in a Czarist officer's uniform, although we found it difficult to keep from chuckling as we remembered him flipping crackers off his nose and trying to catch them in his mouth. Both sang brilliantly.

The next week I received another telephone call from the Opera Association: Our Russian friends desperately wanted to go fishing again and the next evening would be absolutely their last opportunity. Could you possibly . . . ?

Of course I could, so after hasty arrangements Joan set off alone the next afternoon to prepare the cabin while I drove to the Russians' apartment to pick them up. Remembering Nicolai's account of his difficulty obtaining decent fly-tying materials in the Soviet Union, I had hastily raided my extra stocks and swept a few things into a large envelope—some dry-fly hackle, a big patch of deer hair, some chenille, and a few other items. When I reached the apartment, Nicolai appeared wearing a T-shirt with a gigantic illustration of a Royal Coachman fly on the front. I handed him the envelope.

"For me?" he asked, and I nodded. He opened the envelope, looked inside, and his face suddenly had the look of a small boy on Christmas morning. When he looked up again his eyes were misty. "Tank you, tank you, tank you," he said, until I was embarrassed.

Then we set out for the cabin. This time there were no interpreters—just me, Nicolai, Vladimir, and Olga. We conversed as best we could in their limited English and my total ignorance of Russian, and although it was difficult and frustrating at times, we succeeded surprisingly well. The conversation also seemed much more personal and meaningful than talking through an interpreter.

Nicolai and Vladimir managed to make me understand that their temporary fishing licenses had expired and they wanted to get new ones. I tried to explain that I knew the local game warden and was certain there would be no problem in the unlikely event they were checked for licenses, but my assurances were in vain; they were insistent upon being properly licensed. So I began looking for a place that might sell fishing licenses; as it happened, the first one I came to was a Pentagon-size Kmart store.

I found a place in the parking lot and the four of us went in. Nicolai and Vladimir followed me to the sporting-goods department, which was manned by two young jive-talking African American clerks. To say they were amazed to have two Soviet citizens come forward and apply for fishing licenses would be an understatement of the first magnitude. The ensuing conversation—the clerks, amid bursts of laughter, asking questions about the Russians' dates of birth, height, weight, hair and eye color, while Vladimir and Nicolai struggled to understand and respond in a combination of broken English and Russian—was one of the funniest I've ever heard. A sample:

Clerk to Nicolai: "How tall you be, man?"

Nicolai (after a moment's thought): "168."

When the complex transaction was finally complete and we were ready to leave, we discovered Olga was missing. "She probably looking at clothes," Vladimir said, so we headed for the women's clothing department, but she was nowhere to be found.

We started looking up and down the endless aisles of the huge store, but still there was no sign of Olga. I was getting worried, and wondering what to do next, when the salutation "Attention Kmart shoppers!" suddenly came over the store's public-address system. The booming sales pitch gave me an idea: If we could find where the announcements were coming from, perhaps Vladimir could make an appeal to Olga in Russian over the public-address system. I started searching for the source of the announcements, but before we could find it we discovered Olga in the delicatessen department, gazing hungrily at a tray full of sausages. I tried to make her understand that food would be waiting at the cabin, and we gathered her up and left.

From the Kmart we continued north along a busy street rimmed with used-car lots. Most had prices scrawled in greasepaint on their windshields, and this evoked much excited comment from Nicolai and Vladimir. Vladimir looked at the price on the windshield of one battered station wagon, then leaned over the backseat and tapped me on the shoulder. "Excuse me, Stiv," he said, pointing to the station wagon. "They sell without motor?"

Cars remained the subject of conversation as we drove north toward the cabin. This I knew even though Nicolai and Vladimir were speaking rapidly in Russian, for I caught occasional references to "Zheep Sherokees" and "Kadillak El Dorados."

Joan was waiting when we reached the cabin and started to prepare for the fishing. During the Russians' previous visit I had loaned Nicolai and Vladimir each a pair of Korkers—sandals with metal studs on the bottom—to give them better traction on the slippery river rocks. Since then Nicolai had bought his own pair of stream cleats, but I again offered Vladimir a set of Korkers. He declined, but Olga followed me into the cabin, tapped me on the shoulder, and said, "Pliz, Stiv, you put thing on feet." So despite Vladimir's protests, I sat him down, helped him put on the Korkers, and we went fishing.

There had been no rain for weeks and the river was very low, even lower than it had been during the Russians' first visit. The day was also very bright and warm, so I knew our chances of catching anything were poor; nevertheless, we fished hard until it was too dark to see. Nicolai caught and released several more "sardines"—which, with impressive knowledge of steelhead life history, he rightly guessed were smolts, or premigrant steelhead—and hooked another that he allowed Vladimir to play and release. That was because Vladimir again had caught nothing by himself.

We returned to the cabin where we found Joan and Olga carrying on an animated conversation with the aid of a Russian-English dictionary Joan had brought. They had also grilled hamburgers, which we consumed quickly, washing them down with the product of one of the local microbreweries. When he had finished, Nicolai smacked his lips and said: "For me, Amerika is paradise."

After everything was cleaned up and put away, we started back for Seattle with the Russians dozing in the backseat. At their apartment we said our final farewells, with warm and heartfelt embraces all around.

A few nights later, back at the cabin, Joan and I sat next to the river and listened to a live radio broadcast of the final performance of *War and Peace*. Vladimir and Nicolai again sang beautifully, and we listened until the last note died away in the darkness, wondering when—or if—we would ever hear those great voices or see those friendly faces again. None of us had any idea that in little more than a year's time the Soviet Union would cease to exist, that Leningrad would become Saint Petersburg once again, and that the world would be a different, much safer place.

Vladimir and Olga have since emigrated to New York, where Vladimir is now rightfully recognized as one of the leading artists of the Metropolitan Opera. We saw him again briefly on a return trip to Seattle for another singing engagement, but there was no time for fishing. I hope he still has as much enthusiasm for it as he had when we first met.

I suppose Nicolai still lives in Saint Petersburg and fishes the nearby rivers—those not yet ruined by pollution. I trust he was able to tie some useful flies with the materials I gave him. I hope they've brought him some trout larger than sardines.

CHAPTER FOUR

The Last, Best Gift

I was young then and filled with a restless urge to explore new waters. Every creek, every pond, every pool or riffle seemed full of promise, and I wanted to fish them all. To satisfy the urge I spent nights during the week studying maps, noting the locations of waters I hadn't fished; on weekends I would go and try them out.

That was what led me and Ed Foss, my fishing partner, to the Oak Patch. And that was how we met Bill Saunders.

The Oak Patch, a brushy region of second-growth timber in the hills west of Bremerton, is crisscrossed by little streams and freckled with beaver ponds and tiny lakes. You couldn't roam around in that country very long without running across Bill, because that was where he spent most of his time. He was a quiet man with a reserved manner, but if he sized you up and liked what he saw—and if you happened to be carrying fly rods, as we always were—then you quickly became his friend.

Bill lived in Bremerton and wrote an outdoor column for the local newspaper. Mostly he dispensed advice to bait and lure fishermen—tips on where the stocked trout were biting and what sort of unmentionable things people were using to catch them. Sometimes he also offered hints to local fly fishers, although there weren't many at the time, but on most matters related to fly fishing he maintained a strict journalistic silence. That was true even though Bill probably knew as much about the sport as anyone then living in those parts.

What he knew he'd learned mostly the hard way. When he wasn't busy writing his column he was usually out with his fly rod, poking around the brush-cloaked little streams and beer-colored beaver ponds of the Oak Patch. He'd spent decades exploring those hard-to-reach waters, and nobody knew them better.

He kept few fish, but when he did bring one home it was always big—an eye-popping cutthroat, a bright steelhead, sometimes a heavy rainbow or a thick brookie. Occasionally he would tell of other catches, those he hadn't brought home, fish released because he had no need for them. This was long before the idea of catch-and-release caught on, back when very few people let fish go and the few who did were often regarded as if, in terms of mental capacity, they were several eggs short of an omelette. To such derogatory comments Bill paid no attention whatever.

Although he was often willing to talk about the fish he caught, or about fly fishing in general, neither in conversation nor in print would Bill ever reveal just exactly where he fished. He wouldn't even tell Ed or me, although he recognized us as kindred fly-fishing spirits.

Not that he wasn't helpful. Ed and I usually were on the look-out for sea-run cutthroat, and Bill gave us a couple of good clues as to where we could find them. But it was useless to question him about his own favorite spots; he'd just get a twinkle in his eye, smile, and try to change the subject.

Not surprisingly, Bill's angling exploits were frequent topics of local rumor and speculation, and on more than one occasion other fishermen tried to follow him to find out where he fished. Such efforts were always in vain, for Bill had an extraordinary sixth sense that seemed to alert him whenever he was being tailed; he would slip quietly into the thickets and vanish like a ghost, leaving his pursuers empty handed. Some people resented his secrecy, failing to understand how much time and effort he had invested in finding his secret spots and how determined he was to protect his investment. Ed and I understood that part of his nature and respected it; we'd have been secretive, too, under the same circumstances.

Bill was older than either of us, and over the years of our friendship he slowly began to fish less often. The Oak Patch had a way of extracting a physical price from those who tried to fish its waters, and Bill's aging body had reached the point where it could no longer pay the price as easily or as often as it once did. As he became less active Ed and I saw him less frequently; we lived a long distance apart, and our phone calls and visits gradually became fewer.

Then one midwinter day I came home and found an envelope from "B. Saunders" in the mail. I thought as I opened it that it might have been as long as six months since I had last seen or talked to Bill.

Inside the envelope was a single sheet of paper. Unfolded, it revealed a map of the Oak Patch and surrounding countryside, including all the familiar waters I knew well plus quite a few I didn't. What got my attention right away was that some of the latter had been colored in with bright red ink.

That was all. There was no letter or any other explanation.

I was still studying the map when the phone rang. It was Ed.

"I got something very interesting in the mail today," he said.

"So did I."

"A map from Bill Saunders?"

"Yep."

"So he sent us both a copy. I wonder why?"

"Maybe he's just getting too old to fish anymore and finally decided to share his secrets with somebody."

"Maybe so. Anyway, we'll have a lot of fun trying some of these places."

Which we did. When spring came we found our way to one of the ponds inked in red. It was a tough place to reach, screened on all sides by thickets of whippy young alders, ankle-grabbing salal, thorny blackberry, bristling devil's club, and a few stooped and scrawny old firs the loggers had passed over, and it sure didn't look like much when we found it—just a little patch of dark water, barely a long cast from one side to the other, surrounded by floating islands of peat and a jackstraw tangle of old silvery logs. But the pond, if it could be dignified by such a term, quickly yielded a half dozen of the most beautiful cutthroat I've ever seen—plump, olive-yellow, and speckled all over with spots as big and black as those on the flanks of a firehouse dog.

And that was just the first place on the map we visited. Another turned out to be a mysterious little lake that lay hidden in an oval-shaped depression, the afterthought of an ancient glacier, where big trout rose magnificently in the twilight; then there was a stream with a hidden pool where winter steelhead stacked up, and. . . .

But I've almost said too much. It wouldn't do to give away any of Bill's hard-earned secrets.

Of course I meant to call Bill and thank him for the map, but somehow I got distracted and never did—and less than six weeks after it came in the mail I heard that Bill had died.

That was years ago. Now Ed's gone, too, and I suppose my copy of the map is the only one left. It has grown yellow with age, its folds have deepened almost to the point of tatters, and the red ink has begun to fade. But it still reminds me of happy times, of waters I never would have known and fish I never would have caught if the map hadn't led me to them.

It also reminds me of Bill, and each time I look at the map I realize I am looking at an important part of his life, perhaps *the* most important part—the part that became his last, best gift to a pair of fellow anglers he thought might treasure and enjoy his secrets as much as he had.

He was right about that. And somehow I'd like to think he knows I'm grateful, even if I never told him so.

PART II

Places

CHAPTER FIVE

Christmas in January

Banana, Kiritimati—You probably don't recognize this dateline.

Maybe it would help if I told you that Banana is due east of London. Or that Poland lies just a few miles southwest.

That didn't help? Well, perhaps this will: Kiritimati is how the local folks spell Christmas, as in Christmas Island.

The island, a flyspeck of coral and lava, is 119 miles north of the equator and 1,176 miles due south of Hawaii. The villages of Banana, London, and Poland are its main settlements.

Christmas Island is one of the largest coral atolls in the world, but that still doesn't make it very big—about 35 miles from end to end. It was named by the British explorer Captain James Cook, who discovered it on Christmas Eve, 1777. Actually, he didn't discover it so much as it got in his way.

One account says Captain Cook was impressed by how barren the place was. If he were alive today he'd probably still be impressed.

So why would anyone want to come here?

Bonefish.

Back in the early 1980s Christmas Island was found to have perhaps the most concentrated population of bonefish in the world. The bonefish, whose scientific name, *Albula vulpes*, means "white fox," prowls shallow tropical reefs and flats searching for small crabs and shrimp to eat.

As almost every angler knows, the bonefish also is one of the fastest fish in the sea. When hooked on a fly it can take out 150 yards of line and backing in about as much time as it takes to read this paragraph. That's what makes anglers willing to travel to remote destinations to find it.

The Caribbean, from the Bahamas to Venezuela, traditionally has been considered the center of the bonefish universe. But when word got around that Christmas Island also had lots of bones, it suddenly became a popular destination for adventure-minded fishermen.

That was what drew me to Christmas Island, one of a group of seven men and four women fly fishers, including my friend and fishing partner Dave Draheim. We rendezvoused in Honolulu on a January morning in 1989 and made the three-hour flight to Christmas Island aboard a chartered Boeing 737.

We landed on an old military airstrip with grass growing up through cracks in the tarmac. The terminal was a pair of sheds where many laughing island natives were waiting. Christmas Island is visited by no more than a single flight a week, so the plane's arrival is always cause for celebration.

A sign on one of the sheds said the elevation was five feet. Inside we passed a cursory check by a uniformed but barefoot customs inspector, had our passports stamped, then boarded an ancient minibus with rotting, cracked upholstery for the trip to the Captain Cook Hotel. The Captain Cook is a former British Royal Air Force establishment that now caters almost exclusively to visiting anglers (there are hardly any other visitors).

Dave and I were assigned a comfortable beachside bungalow built of flat stones plucked from the surf, mortared together and topped with a steep-pitched, thatched-palm roof. It had a single large room with two beds, storage cabinets, and latticed windows that let the trade winds blow through, keeping the interior temperature surprisingly comfortable. The open windows also admitted the sooth-ing sound of surf breaking on the beach.

A small refrigerator held our daily ration of fresh water. The bathroom had a brackish-water shower and a toilet that worked occasionally. When it did work, it roared and foamed as furiously as the nearby surf.

Our gear had been transported separately from the airstrip in pickup trucks, and as we sorted through it we discovered some of our cargo hadn't made it through customs. The booking agent who had arranged our trip had assured us it would be all right if we brought some beer to supplement the rationed supply of fresh water, so our group had brought five cases of Australian lager. It turned out the booking agent was wrong; all five cases had been seized at the air-port. Bill McIvor, a Bay Area doctor who was the informal head of our group, was advised "negotiations" would be necessary to retrieve the impounded cargo.

Beerless, we got settled in our quarters and then received a briefing from "Big Eddie" Currie, the hotel manager. He explained the daily routine: Guides and fishing locations would be assigned according to a rotation schedule designed to keep each site from being fished more often than once every three days. That was to keep the bonefish from getting excessively spooked.

Breakfast would be served at 5:30 A.M. daily. Then we could each make our own sandwiches for lunch before leaving at 6:30 for the day's fishing. We would fish most of the day, then return to our quarters to freshen up, and everyone would gather in the hotel bar before dinner at 7.

After the briefing we split up into separate groups, climbed into several small Japanese pickup trucks, and headed out to go fishing. The trucks were driven by mahogany-skinned native guides who might have been contenders in the Baja 500. They drove at breakneck speed over crude roads cut through coral and lava beds, bouncing over coconuts, charging through palm thickets, running over scuttling land crabs, sometimes even splashing through saltwater lagoons.

The back of each truck, where we rode, was fitted with benches and an open-sided wooden canopy. A friend who had visited Christmas Island earlier had told me to bring a pillow for the truck—not to sit on, but to wear over my head. Now I understood the reason for his advice: If you sat up straight, your head would hit the canopy with every jolt. We quickly learned to hunker down.

The scenery was fascinating. We drove along the edge of a lagoon where the wind had driven a great lather of foam onto the beach. Round clots of the stuff were splitting off and rolling across the road like snowballs, leaving little wet streaks in their wake. Through the thick brush and coconut palms we glimpsed vast piles of rusting military junk, left over from British and American hydrogen-bomb tests in the late 1950s and early 1960s. The H-bombs were exploded offshore, but the scattered wreckage, along with huge sun-baked flats of dried coral, made it look as if ground zero had been right here on the island.

Big Eddie had told us there were three types of fishing—shore fishing, which meant wading the interior lagoons; "punt" fishing, which meant traveling by boat to coral flats out in the island's main lagoon; and ocean fishing, which meant wading the shallows inside the breaker line.

Dave and I started out shore fishing. Our guide spoke a little English, but when we reached the spot where we were to begin fishing, he hung back and said little. This, we would discover, was typical behavior for nearly all the guides; they served mostly as drivers or boat skippers, taking us to the fishing spots then leaving us pretty much on our own. That was fine with us; we liked figuring things out for ourselves. But along with some other members of our party, neither Dave nor I had ever fished for bonefish before, and in retrospect we might have fared better with a little more help from the guides.

As it was, we started wading and searching for fish on our own. It didn't take long to confirm the truth of everything I'd heard about bonefish being difficult to see; their silver flanks and faint-green-barred backsides gave them almost perfect camouflage, even in the air-clear water over the snow-white coral flats we were wading. Even with polarized sunglasses it was hard to see fish, especially when clouds passed over the sun or wind ruffled the water, as they did most of the time.

Nevertheless, we did see some. That was when we learned that seeing them was only half the battle; we had to stalk them, too, quietly and carefully, then cast so our fly settled gently into the water, without creating a disturbance; otherwise the fish would spook. Even if we did all these things successfully, there was no guarantee a fish would take.

I cast to 12 or 15 fish that first afternoon. Several followed my fly, one took it and I missed the strike, and another grabbed the fly but came loose just as I got it on the reel. The only fish I landed was a little yellow snapper about half the size of a football. Dave had a more successful start, hooking two bonefish, including a beautiful 6-pounder he landed after a 20-minute fight with seven trips into the backing. He was blooded; I was not.

Next morning we walked to breakfast under a brilliant canopy of stars, including the Southern Cross. Afterward we made sandwiches for lunch, choosing from a limited selection of peanut butter and jelly or ham and cheese on bread baked locally with coconut milk (sweet but very good). Then Dave and I joined Dan and

Barbara Reid for a bumpy pickup-truck ride to the town of London, a shabby cluster of Quonset huts, cinder-block houses, and other patchwork structures near the entrance to the main lagoon. There we boarded one of the island's punts, a large outboard-powered wooden craft with open sides and a roof. Following the guide's suggestion, we all rode on the roof to avoid being soaked with spray while the punt crossed the choppy open water of the lagoon.

After a long run the guide stopped the punt and anchored on a shallow flat, where we got out to wade and fish. Conditions were far from ideal; the wind was blowing strongly and dark clouds hid the sun and discharged occasional spatters of rain. Oddly, the raindrops evaporated the moment they struck, so we never got wet.

Despite the weather, I sighted, hooked, and landed my first bonefish that morning. It ran with speed and strength that seemed far beyond its size, a kind of ruthless energy I had never felt from any freshwater fish. That one was followed by ten more before the day was out, each as wild and strong as the first. All my expectations were fulfilled or exceeded; truly these were incredible fish.

Well satisfied, I rejoined the others and we punted back to London in late afternoon, then returned to the Captain Cook Hotel. The first order of business upon arrival was to change clothes and rinse out our gear. We had waded wet in cotton trousers and tennis shoes, and while the wading was pleasant, it had been virtually impossible to keep coral sand from getting inside our shoes. After a while the accumulated grit had become a little uncomfortable, a bit like walking through a pile of sawdust in low-cut shoes, but a double layer of socks had kept the tiny coral slivers from penetrating the soles of our feet. Still, it took a lot of rinsing to remove the stuff from our socks.

Later everyone gathered in the hotel bar to compare notes on the day's fishing. There we also learned that negotiations over our impounded beer were proceeding slowly; apparently diplomacy on any level simply can't be rushed. Meanwhile, we were told, if we wanted a glass of beer we could buy one at the hotel bar.

That announcement made everything clear: When the customs officials had seen our cargo of beer on the airplane, they had grown alarmed at the possible loss of a week's revenue from the hotel bar. So they had solved the problem by seizing our beer.

In the end, after another day of negotiations, we ransomed the beer by passing the hat and raising $82, which was paid to a customs official (he called it "duty"). By then, however, there wasn't time enough left for us to drink all of it, so the natives ended up with some of it anyway.

Cocktail-hour entertainment at the hotel consisted of watching geckos (lizards) run up and down the mirror behind the bar. Then we adjourned to the dining room for the evening meal. The food was good, if you like fish. We had steamed fish, broiled fish, fish wrapped in cabbage, stewed fish, blackened fish, and barbecued fish, not to mention lobster, octopus, and squid.

After dinner one evening I went for a walk, determined to see more of the island. The steady wind rattled palm fronds and brought the scent of cooking fires, food, and other less pleasant odors from the nearby village. Wreckage was scattered everywhere—skeletons of trucks, fuel tanks, and other unidentifiable twisted metal objects, all strewn among the concrete foundations of vanished buildings. It made an eerie scene in the evening light, like the landscape from a science-fiction movie depicting a postnuclear nightmare. In a sense that's what it was.

Christmas Island has a strange history. Like most atolls, it began as a thumb of lava pushing its way up from the Pacific floor to the surface. Then, over ages, countless coral polyps added their limestone skeletons to the lava foundations, slowly creating the out-line of the atoll as it is today—a maze of sandy islands centered on a large lagoon. The atoll is shaped roughly like a pork chop, with the lagoon inside its larger end. Its maximum elevation, atop a sand dune, is 35 feet.

Except for millions of seabirds and thousands of turtles, the atoll was deserted when Captain Cook discovered it. The first recorded residents, in the early 1800s, were survivors of ships that foundered in the Bay of Wrecks east of Christmas Island. They stayed until someone rescued them—or until they died.

In 1858, the United States annexed Christmas Island under the American Guano Act, a measure authorizing extraction of bird guano (for fertilizer) from uninhabited Pacific islands. But the atoll's guano deposits proved too scattered for commercial exploitation.

Employees of a New Zealand company settled the island next, in 1882. They collected shells for buttons and harvested copra (dried coconut meat) from coconut palms. But those ventures didn't work out, either, and soon the island was abandoned again.

In 1911 it was resettled by immigrants from other Pacific islands and has been occupied ever since. Between World Wars I and II it became more or less the private preserve of a Frenchman named Petrics Rougier, who put other immigrants to work on his coconut plantations and built a home he called Paris.

During World War II the island became a center for Allied air operations in the South Pacific, but no fighting took place there.

Then, in 1957, Britain chose Christmas Island for nuclear tests. The United States joined in a few years later. The two powers brought in fleets of vehicles and heavy equipment and built airfields, a network of paved roads, hundreds of buildings, power plants, pipelines, communications networks, towers, bunkers, tennis courts, officers' clubs, and so on. Then they exploded about 30 H-bombs off the shore of the island.

In 1964, they all went home. Most of what they had brought with them was left behind to rust and decay—an incredible fortune in abandoned equipment and buildings. Your tax dollars at work.

A British commissioner took over administration of the island and refused to let natives use the vehicles or live in the abandoned buildings. Those who tried to scavenge materials for their own use were caught and sent off the island.

The leftover military junk slowly rusted and crumbled in the fury of ocean storms. Much of it also was dismembered, burned, or otherwise destroyed by vengeful natives. Now the island is covered from end to end with rusting vehicles and other junk.

In 1979, Christmas Island became part of the new Republic of Kiribati (pronounced KIR-i-boss), a confederation of 33 small islands scattered over two million miles of ocean. The capital, Tarawa, where U.S. Marines fought a bloody battle against the Japanese in World War II, is more than 2,000 miles west of Christmas Island.

The people who live on Christmas Island today are mostly of Micronesian or Polynesian descent. They speak I-Kiribati, a vowel-heavy Gilbert Islands dialect, but most also know at least some English.

Christmas Island is viewed as something of a land of opportunity by the citizens of Kiribati, one of the poorest nations on earth. The island has more food than most others in the republic, and its copra plantations and commercial fisheries provide jobs and a chance to save a little money (since there's virtually no place on the island to spend it). So in recent years Christmas Island has seen an influx of new residents, especially from Tarawa.

Most of these new arrivals live in the villages of London, Banana, and Poland. Some dwell in cinder-block houses, either newly built or left over from the military occupation. Many live in huts made from scraps of aluminum salvaged from Quonset huts or airplane hangars. Bicycles are the principal mode of transportation on the island, although a few motor vehicles ply the military roads. Fallen coconuts pose a constant road hazard.

Village stores stock mostly canned goods, locally baked bread, and other staples. Occasionally they offer unexpected items, such as Michael Jackson T-shirts.

Without the coconut palm, life on Christmas Island would be impossible. Palm fibers and logs provide construction materials. Coconuts provide food, milk, and copra for export, and their husks serve as fuel for cooking fires. Sap from the coconut is used to make toddy, the local native beverage.

The island way of life is still primitive by most standards. But there are jarring signs of modern influence. As I walked around, I saw a sarong-clad native woman building a cooking fire while she listened to rock music from a Sony Walkman. Teenagers walked past with boom boxes glued to their ears. A native clad in a traditional ceremonial costume made of palm fronds paused to look at his Rolex watch. Christmas Island is a place of many contrasts.

With all these impressions crowding my mind, I returned to the bungalow and fell asleep to the deep murmur of the surf.

The next several days were busy with bonefish. Most we hooked were small—1 to 2 pounds—but even fish of that size routinely took 20 yards of backing on their first runs. We also caught good numbers of fish weighing 5 to 7 pounds, and these often ran as far as 150 yards on their initial burst. All were released. Local regulations require anglers to use barbless hooks and release all bonefish, a wise policy that should assure good fishing at Christmas Island for many years to come.

Snappers and small jacks added occasional variety, and one day a 2-$^1/_2$-foot blacktip shark took my fly and put up a stout fight before I brought it close enough to cut the leader, carefully avoiding its formidable array of teeth.

The flies we used were variations of the Crazy Charlie, surely the world's most popular bonefish fly. Pink and gold were the most effective colors, although it took a little experimenting to find which color the bonefish preferred each day. Floating lines and long leaders were mandatory in the shallow, clear water.

The large flats in the main lagoon offered the most action and the biggest fish. They seemed almost endless, stretching to the horizon like the Mojave Desert covered by a thin layer of water. To wade alone on one of these great expanses, surrounded by vast distances of sky and water, was a humbling experience.

One afternoon while wading one of these flats I hooked a big bonefish whose repeated long runs caused a backlash in the backing on my reel. Rather than waste time trying to untangle the snarl, I switched to a backup reel rigged with a brand-new fly line. Moments later I hooked another bonefish that made a characteristically strong first run, but I recovered most of the line and backing. All seemed well when the fish started its second run. Suddenly the line went slack and I saw that the backing knot had parted and the fish was running off with my new fly line.

I splashed after it across the flat, trying to keep the fly line in sight—not an easy task considering the line was white and the bottom was, too. The fish paused briefly and I was able to catch up and grab hold of the line, but just as quickly the fish pulled it from my grasp and was off again. Resuming the chase, I caught up to the line again; this time the bonefish obligingly waited while I passed the end of the line twice through the buttoned rod-holder loop on my fishing shirt to secure it. Then, while the fish tugged occasionally on the other end, I tried desperately to rejoin the line to the backing. The first attempt failed—the knot pulled out—but the second resulted in a firm connection (and possibly a world speed record for tying the Albright special knot). When the knot was finished I unbuttoned the rod-holder loop on my shirt to free the line, reeled in the slack, and restored the connection to the fish—which, amazingly, was still on. I landed it a few moments later.

Smoky Flat at the far southwest end of the main lagoon provided some of the most exciting fishing. Surrounded by deep water, the flat was crisscrossed by shallow tidal channels that feeding bonefish used to come and go. We learned to stake out these channels near the edge of the flat and wait for bonefish to come in from the depths.

That was how I intercepted my first big fish, a 6-pounder. Seeing the fish enter the channel, I dropped my fly well ahead of it, waited until the fish reached the spot, then twitched the fly once. The bone pounced on it immediately and I set the hook firmly. The fish ripped off 150 yards of backing on its first run, a gleaming missile that took 15 minutes to land.

Later, on the same flat, I saw a big dinner-plate-shaped fish coming toward me at freeway speed, the top half of its sickle-shaped tail slicing through the surface and throwing up a rooster-tail wake like a small hydroplane. It was a big white trevally, and when I cast the fish turned obediently, took my fly, and I hooked it squarely.

For a moment the trevally seemed unconcerned. Then all hell broke loose; the fish dashed away in a blur, leaving what looked like a trail of smoke through the water. First it ran one way, then another, taking my line around a coral head. There was a loud snap, then the line went slack. I was lucky to get everything back but the fly.

That fish might have weighed 25 or 30 pounds. Later I hooked a smaller one, probably about 10 pounds, which also escaped with my fly. Nobody in our party succeeded in landing a trevally larger than 5 pounds; with our light bonefish tackle, we were undermatched for these muscular fish.

The inshore flats offered smaller bonefish and fewer trevally, but many more birds. Brazen frigate birds and brown boobies hovered around us while we fished, making us afraid of hooking one on a backcast, and sometimes they dropped to the surface and tried to take our flies. Less annoying and far more graceful were the smaller sooty and fairy terns that swirled overhead.

Although we saw birds in huge numbers, we were told the island's bird life is much less abundant now than before the nuclear tests. Countless millions of birds were blinded by the flash of exploding H-bombs and later died. Many others died young after pigs and cats were introduced on the island and began raiding vulnerable nests in the low-lying scrub. With as many birds as there are now, it's difficult to imagine what things must have been like before these setbacks.

Time spent fishing always seems to go faster than time spent any other way, and almost before we knew it our last morning was at hand. Dave and I climbed into the back of a pickup and held on with white knuckles while the guide drove off the road and bushwhacked through palm thickets and over fallen coconuts until we finally emerged on a coral ridge overlooking the ocean. Glad to escape from the truck, we scampered down the gentle slope to begin fishing the shallow water inside the breaker line.

This fishing was different. Incoming waves, backlit by the sun, glowed alternately lavender, purple, and turquoise, then crested suddenly in whiteness and broke against the coral, creating wreaths of foam that washed toward us and curled like white smoke around our feet. In the great noise of breaking waves we could hear the beat of the heavy engine of the earth, a deep, hollow, constant bass that filled the air until there was no room left for any other sound. In sequence with the breaking waves, the water rose quickly from our ankles to above our knees, filling the swale between the outer layers of coral and the beach. Within that flooded gap were fish of all kinds, including some of the largest bonefish we had seen.

In this wild place of contending sounds and waters I quickly hooked and landed a 5-pounder and lost three other good fish that ran out through the breakers into deep water and escaped. Then a pretty little bluefin trevally came to my fly, followed by a strong, heavy fish that took all my line and nearly all my backing on a long, powerful run far beyond the breakers. Sharp coral heads loomed everywhere and the chances of recovering my line—let alone the leader, fly, and fish—seemed nil. But the fish was well hooked and the line somehow stayed free of the coral.

Leaning into the rod as hard as I dared, I managed to recover a little line, only to have the fish take it out again in strong runs that tore skin from my knuckles when I tried to slow the rapidly turning reel. The struggle went on for what seemed a long time and still we had not been able to see or identify the fish, which had spent the whole time in deep water on the other side of the reef. Finally I felt it begin to tire and eased it slowly through an opening in the coral until at last it was circling close in the shallow water. Only then did we have our first clear view of it.

"Sweet lips," the guide said. "Very good to eat."

I didn't know what a "sweet lips" was, but seeing the guide's delight I quickly offered him the fish. His grin was even wider than the one on the fish's ugly face. "My family eat," he said happily as he hoisted the fish from the water.

Much later I learned sweet lips was the local name for a long-nosed emperorfish. By any name, it was one of the toughest fish I'd ever tangled with. It was also my last at Christmas Island.

That night we were treated to a luau with roast pig, lobsters grilled over a coconut-husk fire, many kinds of fish, octopus, salads, and cheese bread. Then a native troupe entertained with songs and an elaborate dance chant that went on for more than 40 minutes. When it was over they presented each of us a wreath of fragrant blossoms. If all this was intended to make us feel good about coming back to Christmas Island, it had its desired effect.

Next morning the 737 arrived with a new contingent of anglers and our party boarded for the flight back to Honolulu. As the jet lifted off the long airstrip I kept my eyes glued to a window, straining for a last look at Christmas Island, somehow feeling connected to it for as long as I could still see it. From the air the startling blue water of the lagoon contrasted brilliantly with the blinding white sand of the great flats, a symbol of the many contrasts on Christmas Island. There was a last glimpse of the narrow islands rimming the atoll, coconut palms swaying in the breeze while row upon row of white-capped swells marched steadily toward their sandy beaches. Then it all vanished beneath a layer of cloud and the connection was broken.

Many hours later I stepped off the plane into a blizzard in Seattle, and suddenly Christmas Island seemed a very long way off in both space and time. But I'll always remember it as one of the best Christmases I've ever had.

CHAPTER SIX

Dee Days

Long before dawn on the first morning I was to fish the River Dee I was awakened by the wind. Outside the cottage it was whistling and shrieking with wild strength, and along with it I could hear a steady thumping sound.

Maybe it was the rabbits, I thought. All of northern Scotland is undermined with rabbit tunnels, and there are probably more of the furry little beasts in the country than there are humans. The day before, in the fields around the cottage, I had seen whole regiments of rabbits; now I supposed maybe the wind was blowing them against the side of the house.

It had been blowing steadily for five days, ever since I'd landed at Glasgow, but before it had merely been a gale; now it was more like a hurricane. Looking through the cottage window at first light, I could see trees bent parallel to the ground, rapidly shedding limbs and leaves, while great waves of wind flattened the surrounding fields of grass and grain.

I went back to bed and tried to sleep, but the roar of wind and the constant thumping kept me awake. At last, when the light was full, I got up and went outside to see if there was a pile of dead rabbits on the windward side of the cottage. There wasn't—something else must have been thumping—but that was no fault of the wind; it seemed to be getting even stronger.

It was almost pointless to think of going fishing. But when one has a chance to fish a storied river like the Aberdeenshire Dee, one does so, no matter what the weather.

I had come to Scotland with my family, the trip a college gradu-
ation present for my daughter. We had spent the past several days
working our way slowly northeastward from Glasgow and
Edinburgh, taking time to explore ruined castles, old forts, stone cir-
cles and other antiquities. Our destination was the resort town of
Ballater on the Dee, where we had been invited by Cliff Jefferies, a
retired British Army colonel, and his wife, Maureen, to stay at
Tomnakiest, their hillside residence overlooking the river.

The invitation had been welcome but unexpected, since I had
never met Colonel Jefferies. We had a mutual friend, Frank Webster,
who had served in the colonel's regiment, and when I asked Frank for
advice on how to arrange fishing on the Dee, he had gotten in touch
with the colonel. The result was a letter inviting us to stay at
Tomnakiest; Colonel Jefferies even generously offered to arrange my
fishing and loan me his tackle so I would not have to bring my own.

The colonel proved to be a tall, handsome, well-built man with
the erect posture and no-nonsense manner of a career military officer. He and his wife greeted us warmly upon our arrival at
Tomnakiest and showed us to our quarters, then invited us for cocktails after we were settled. When we joined them I asked about his
military career; he told me he had been a bomb-disposal officer
whose far-flung assignments had included removing unexploded ord-
nance from the Pacific battlefields of Tarawa and Guadalcanal. His
last duty assignment before his retirement 12 years earlier had been
as personal bodyguard to the Prince of Wales, which had given him
the opportunity to become well acquainted with the Royal Family.
This had earned him a place on the regular invitation list for events
at nearby Balmoral Castle when the Royal Family was in residence.
He was, I thought, a very well-connected man; no wonder he had
been able to arrange my fishing.

During his retirement Colonel Jefferies said he also had owned and operated three different shops in Ballater, including a fishing shop. That shop had since been sold, but he casually mentioned that he still supplied most of the trout and salmon flies for the commercial trade in northern Scotland.

"As a matter of fact," he said, "I have about 400,000 flies upstairs in my loft right now; would you like to see them?"

I could only nod, dumbfounded at the thought of so many flies. He led the way up a flight of stairs to a loft rimmed with wooden chests filled with narrow drawers, which he began opening one by one. Each drawer held scores of flies of every color, size, and shape. There were trout flies tied on single hooks and salmon flies tied on doubles, all of the highest quality, and the colonel said they were made for him by a regular cadre of tiers with whom he did business. It was an amazing display, and after seeing the contents of all those drawers I had little doubt the colonel had been close to the mark when he said he had 400,000 flies.

The next morning—the morning of the wind—we met after breakfast and drove down to the river in the colonel's Range Rover, bucking heavy gusts every inch of the way. En route the colonel explained that he had arranged for me to fish two days on the Monaltrie Water, a mile-long beat on the north side of the Dee just downstream from Ballater.

He stopped at a ghillie's hut next to a fine-looking run he identified as Mitchell's Pool, which he said was near the head of the Monaltrie Water. Then he got out his tackle from the back of the Rover, including a 15-1/4-foot double-handed rod—standard issue for the Dee, but a rod with one more handle and 6-1/4 feet more length than any I'd ever used before. Matched to a 10-weight floating line, it felt like a utility pole when I hefted it. The river wasn't much larger than my home river, the North Fork of the Stillaguamish in Washington State, where I often fish with a 7-foot rod and a 6-weight line. Colonel Jefferies's rig appeared gigantic by comparison, out of scale for such a small river.

That seemed even more true when he handed me a selection of wet flies tied on size 10 or 12 double hooks. The river was low and clear, he said, and under those circumstances such small, dark patterns were best.

He took up the big double-handed rod and demonstrated how to handle it, making several long, apparently effortless casts. Then he handed me the rod so I could try it while he watched with a critical eye; my casts were shorter and required plenty of effort.

The colonel explained that the ghillie responsible for the beat was away, helping investigate an accident somewhere up in the hills, and the colonel himself had other business, so I would have to fish alone. He advised me to cast across or slightly quartering downstream, mend line as necessary, and let the fly swing through the field of vision of any salmon that might be lying in wait. Then he wished me well, got into the Rover, and drove off, leaving me alone on the river.

I started in near the top of Mitchell's Pool where a fine narrow tongue of water broke into a broad section of deeper, quiet water that seemed pregnant with possibilities. The wind was still screaming—I guessed its speed at a steady 30 or 40 miles an hour with gusts as high as 60—and foam-flecked waves danced across the pool. I felt a little ridiculous using a 15-1/4-foot rod to throw a size 12 fly, but in the teeth of that fearsome gale I soon began to appreciate the properties of such a big weapon; it might have been difficult to cast with anything less. Still, I had difficulty mastering the big rod; like everything else in fly fishing, it was a matter of timing, not to be learned easily in a single day during a high wind.

Despite the wind, the day was sunny and clear, which made the water easy to read and the wading pleasant. As I grew comfortable with the river's strength and feel, I also began to appreciate its surroundings. An artificial forest stood on the far side of the river, with pine trees arranged in neat rows like soldiers in ranks, all the same size. On my side there was mostly pasture, heavily populated with cattle, but the cattle were massively outnumbered by the ubiquitous rabbits.

Every earthen bank, every grassy ledge, every hummock was pocked with rabbit holes, rabbit runs, rabbit town houses, and rabbit condos. As I walked between pools, scores of rabbits would sit and watch my approach, then scramble into their holes when I drew near, only to re-emerge after I passed and watch me walk away. It looked as if I had stumbled onto the Tokyo or Mexico City of rabbitdom, the universal center of rabbit culture, the place where headquarters will be established if rabbits ever take over the world. Someday, I thought, a rabbit is going to dig a tunnel too far, and all of northern Scotland will cave in.

But there was other wildlife to be seen as well—a roe deer peering through the pine trees on the far side of the river, oystercatchers perched on rocks in the river, stately herons lifting off on ungainly wings, and the local version of the merganser, flying low in bulletlike trajectories.

I had plenty of time to see all these things as I worked my way downstream, for the wind forced me to fish slowly. It was necessary to wait for a lull between gusts before I dared lift line off the river to make another cast, and even then a new gust would sometimes catch the line in midair and blow it directly downstream, which meant waiting for another lull to try again. It was hard, painstaking work.

After a couple of hours a particularly violent gust tore the hat off my head and sent it sailing downstream; I could only watch helplessly as it tumbled end over end until it finally fell to the surface and vanished in a distant riffle. Needless to say, it was one of my favorite fishing hats; its loss also exposed the widening gap in the hair on top of my head, but fortunately I had thought to bring along a bottle of sunblock. A liberal application took care of the problem.

The river was full of fish—mostly grilse but also a few salmon. I saw at least one roll or leap in every pool, including a couple of salmon of 20 pounds or more. Fixing their locations, I fished over them patiently, changing flies until I had used all the patterns the colonel had given me, but there were no takes.

After seven hours of fishing my score was no fish hooked, one hat lost. My right wrist ached badly from the big rod and I longed for calm weather, one of my own little rods, and a dry fly. The way those fish were rolling, I was convinced they could have been taken with a dry. Just then, however, I was even more convinced of the need for dinner and a good night's sleep to prepare for my second round on the Dee.

The Dee is unique among Scottish salmon rivers in its origin, a spring known as the Wells of Dee. The spring is located near the rocky summit of the Cairngorms, Scotland's highest mountain range, and its flow spills downward through a remote pass known as Lairig Ghru. Below the pass it joins Gharbh Choire Burn, the first of many tributaries, serpentines its way through the Cairngorm Nature Reserve, past the Forest of Mar, then turns eastward toward the North Sea. It plunges over a succession of small waterfalls called the Linn of Dee, accepts the water of more tributaries, and finally assumes the character and shape that have made it world famous as a salmon river.

Past the town of Braemar the river enters a lovely valley that carries it downstream to Balmoral Castle, where the Queen Mother and her ghillie have long been familiar figures on the stream. Downstream from Balmoral it is joined by two more large tributaries, the Gairn and the Muick, just before it reaches Ballater. Ballater itself is Scotland's equivalent of Aspen, Colorado, a picturesque resort town with quaint, expensive shops, tearooms, hotels, and excellent restaurants.

Below Ballater, on a hillside almost within view of the spot where I lost my hat, are the remains of an ancient stone church founded by Saint Nathan, a kindly soul who raised vegetables and shared them with the local peasants. Saint Nathan is the source of a River Dee legend.

One summer, the legend goes, there was a prolonged spell of bad weather that threatened Nathan's vegetable crop, frustrating the good man to the point that he eventually lost his temper and started cursing the weather. Realizing this was bad form for a holy man, Nathan was overcome with remorse and chose a rather extreme method of penance: He handcuffed his right arm to his right leg, then threw the key into the River Dee (a neat trick if he was right handed). Thus shackled, he started for Rome to seek forgiveness directly from the pope, traveling the whole way with his arm handcuffed to his leg. Upon his arrival in Rome he was welcomed with a meal of fresh fish, and when he sliced open the first one—you guessed it—there in its stomach was the key to his handcuffs.

And if you believe that story, then you'll believe that when I return to the North Fork of the Stillaguamish I'll catch a steelhead with my lost hat in its stomach.

My second day on the Dee also was my birthday and I celebrated by driving into Ballater and buying a new Hardy fishing hat to replace the one I had lost. Then I drove to the river, ate lunch at the ghillie's hut, and started fishing the same beat I'd fished the day before. The gale-force winds had subsided a bit and in their absence I was somewhat better able to master the idiosyncrasies of the long rod and heavy line, although they still felt like brutes compared to my usual light tackle.

Even more salmon were visible in the river than on the first day and their restless behavior and the nature of the water again made me think a dry fly might be the answer. But there were no dries in the selection of flies the colonel had given me, and when I met other anglers fishing the adjoining beats and asked about dry flies the conversation usually went something like this:

Me: "Do these salmon ever take a dry fly?"

Local Angler (giving me a funny look): "Oh dear me, no."

Me: "Have you ever tried fishing a dry fly?"

Local Angler (another funny look): "Well, of course not!"

Me: "Why not?"

Local Angler: "Because these salmon won't take a dry fly!"

And that seemed to be that.

So I stuck with my borrowed tackle and borrowed tactics. I fished through Mitchell's Pool three times, losing count of the number of fish I saw jumping there—including one grilse that came out of the water within ten feet of where I was standing—then moved downstream to fish Kate's Pool and another pool below that. By then evening was coming on quickly, and with my time on the river fast running out I hastened back to Mitchell's for one last try, fishing until it was dark at 8 P.M. and I was weary from walking and wading and using the heavy rod.

I suppose you're wondering if I ever did catch a salmon that day. Well, the answer is yes. It was silvery and bright, covered with a fine spray of spots and little red freckles, and it measured about six inches long—a salmon parr yet to make its first journey to the sea.

And that was all. My only consoling thought was that if you're going to get skunked, it may as well be on a classic, storied river like the Dee. Fish or no fish, I was grateful for the chance to experience this famous water and its beautiful surroundings, grateful too for the hospitality of the local people and the wonderful generosity of my hosts.

But next time, if there is one, I'll bring some dry flies. And maybe I'll catch a fish more than six inches long.

CHAPTER SEVEN

On the Edge of
the Earth

Among the volcanic footprints that stretch across the southern Caribbean Sea is a bright little necklace of islands known collectively as Turneffe Island. A classic atoll, it encloses a bewildering number of amoeba-shaped, low-lying landforms covered thickly with sprawling mangroves. For ages the jumbled fire-hose roots of these aggressive plants have been at work trapping their own dead leaves and other organic materials to create new soil, making the islands grow; their shapes and sizes are also sometimes more quickly and dramatically altered by passing hurricanes.

The overall shape of Turneffe Island was established long ago by volcanic action, and if you look at a map you will see that its outline resembles a human foot. At the northern end is the rounded heel; at the southern end are the toes, in the form of a labyrinth of tiny islands. There is even an arch in the middle of the foot, separating two large interior lagoons. A reef adds definition, extending nearly all the way around the outer edge of the atoll. Beyond the reef the bottom drops away quickly to deep water; inside are miles of shallow, sunbaked flats.

None of this is apparent, however, when you approach the archipelago by boat. From that vantage point Turneffe Island first appears as a hedge of green foliage looming from a crystal sea. These are the mangroves, first over the horizon, and they cover every scrap of land with a seemingly impenetrable wall of roots, limbs, and leaves. Only when you approach closely can you see there are gaps in this green monolith, a series of narrow, inward-leading creeks and passes. One of these leads to a sandy islet called Little Caye Bokel, which looks like a lump of white sugar crowned with mangroves, coconut palms, and sea grapes. And there, sitting on top of it like the decoration on a wedding cake, is Turneffe Island Lodge.

As fly-fishing destinations go, Turneffe Island has been around a long time—long enough, perhaps, for some of its luster to wear off. The great bonefish populations that made it popular in the 1960s and 1970s were decimated by unrestricted net fishing, and only when it became apparent that a valuable resource was being lost did the Belizian government step in to ban the nets. At first the ban accomplished little because it was not enforced, but then the government belatedly started cracking down. Now most of the nets are gone and the bonefish populations have had an opportunity to recover in both size and numbers.

The fortunes of Turneffe Island Lodge have pretty much followed those of the bonefish. It changed hands several times and was in rather run-down condition when Dallas Gay and his sons, Tommy and Jeff, of Gainesville, Georgia, purchased it in March 1995. They began refurbishing the lodge with the goal of re-establishing it as a pre-eminent fly-fishing destination, and after 15 months of work decided it was time to show off what they had done. I was among six anglers invited to see the improvements and sample the fishing.

The 30-mile boat trip from Belize City on the mainland to the lodge took nearly two hours. We followed a southeasterly course through an opening in the world's second-longest barrier reef until we finally came within sight of the mangrove hedge that marks the western edge of the Turneffe Archipelago. When we arrived in late afternoon Tommy Gay was on hand to greet us. A likable young man with a soft southern drawl, he introduced me to the other fishermen, most of whom had arrived earlier, and we all got acquainted over dinner.

Next morning Tommy and I loaded our fly rods and gear aboard one of the lodge's new 16-foot Super Dolphin skiffs, skippered by Nick Bardalez, a veteran guide. Nick steered the skiff at high speed through a tangled network of narrow mangrove creeks and passes until we emerged at the edge of a broad, cream-colored flat, which Nick identified as Calabash Flat. He staked out the skiff and Tommy and I picked up our rods and stepped over the side into the warm water.

The morning was sunny and bright, although clouds hung on the horizon like great clusters of dark purple grapes. Ospreys glided overhead, pelicans rode past on the breeze, and herons stepped purposefully through the shallows near the mangrove roots as we followed Nick across the flat. A steady breeze ruffled the water, creating a colorful, ever-changing *craquelure* on the surface. The air was warm and moist.

Nick shaded his eyes as he waded, looking for bonefish. Each step into the soft marl of the flat stirred up little clouds of silt from the bottom, and I soon felt the familiar grit of coral sand inside my shoes.

We had gone only a little way when Nick stopped and raised his arm. I looked where he was pointing; the sea ahead glittered with a thousand points of light, metallic reflections from a host of little saber shapes flashing in the sun. Bonefish tails! It was the largest school of bonefish I'd ever seen.

I felt a familiar surge of excitement as I stripped line from my reel, crouched low, and tiptoed through the turtle grass to get within casting range of the school. My first cast was ignored, but the second was seized by an angry bonefish that started instantly on a high-speed dash across the flat. For a few moments I was serenaded by the sweet music of my reel; then the hook pulled out.

The same thing happened with the next fish I hooked, and the one after that. But it didn't matter, because there were plenty more where these came from, and Tommy and I spent the morning exercising bonefish until we were weary. Years had passed since I'd last felt the electric thrill of a bonefish on its first wild run; feeling it again renewed my admiration and respect for the amazing strength and power of these fish.

That evening over dinner there was much excited talk about the day's fishing and the promise of the days ahead, but the physical exertions of a long day of wading, casting, and playing fish under a hot sun had made everyone weary, and the dining room and bar were empty by shortly after 9.

After a good night's sleep in an air-conditioned room, it was something of a shock to step outside the next morning; the temperature already was in the high eighties although it was not yet 7 o'clock. But by the time breakfast was over a steady breeze was blowing, making the air temperature comfortable. With Joe Faber as our guide, I joined Gary Merriman, owner of an Atlanta fly-fishing shop, and we ran to a place called Big Flat, where Joe staked out the skiff and pointed out a huge school of bonefish moving along the reef.

Gary and I got out and waded after them, casting into the densely packed school, which held hundreds of fish. It was almost like fishing in a hatchery, except the fish were restless and nervous. At first they refused every fly we threw at them.

We followed them a long way, casting repeatedly and changing flies often, hoping to find a pattern they would take. At length Gary hooked a fish that made a strong run; when it stopped Gary turned it and began to recover line. Then suddenly the fish took off on a second run even stronger than the first. We soon saw the reason for its panic: The bonefish had a barracuda on its tail. The race was short and the barracuda won, swallowing the whole rear half of the bonefish in a single bloody gulp.

A short while later I had a take from a good fish that I fought for a long time in the shallow water over the reef until it finally broke my leader on a sharp piece of coral. And those were the only two fish we managed to entice from the school.

But our trek along the reef had been rewarding in other ways. As the morning sun edged higher, the ragged coral ridges and nearby flats were illuminated as brilliantly as if they had their own mysterious inner source of light, and they glowed with all the colors of the spectrum—rich cream and dark cobalt, turquoise and azure blue, lavender and red, and the deepest of all greens.

The reef also came alive with the quick movements of its many inhabitants. Brilliant doctorfish darted through the shallows while schools of large parrotfish displayed palettes of bright color as they came in cautiously to feed. Needlefish glided over the surface for incredible distances like silver darts, schools of minnows burst out of the water like bright raindrops in reverse, and great dark rays moved across the flats with slow wing beats, leaving swirls of turbidity in their wakes. The shadowy shapes of prowling sharks were sometimes visible, along with odd silver-green boxfish, floppy-finned triggerfish, and a host of other teeming, restless forms of life.

Wading the reef was like walking on the edge of the earth. Lazy, white-tipped breakers spilled their energy almost at our feet; beyond them was the ocean, stretching endlessly toward a magic meeting point of sky and water. From somewhere out there came the wind and waves, each wave driven by the pulsing energy of the world's great hidden heart until it died on the multicolored reef. There are many kinds of beauty in the world, but few that match or exceed the beauty of a tropical reef.

The scenery was hypnotic, but Joe reminded us our purpose was to find fish, and when we could not find any more along the reef he suggested it was time to move on. We returned to the skiff; Joe started the motor and headed for a place called Fabian's Flat, where we found another large school of bonefish. Joe staked out the skiff and Gary and I got out and started stalking the school on foot until we were within casting distance, but as I double-hauled to make my first cast the fly line suddenly came apart in my hands. I realized then that the bonefish that earlier had broken me over the sharp coral also had damaged my fly line.

I had brought along a backup reel, an old Hardy, and exchanged it for the one with the broken line. But the Hardy fit awkwardly on the reel seat of the rod I was using, and a few minutes later, when I hooked a bonefish, the reel flew off and landed in the water. Fortunately the fish was not large and I was able to strip line by hand and land it despite the handicap. Then I retrieved the reel, cleaned the coral sand out of it, and this time made sure it was securely fastened to the rod.

The next fish I hooked was landed without mishap, which seemed a change for the better, but after that we had no further activity until late afternoon. By then Gary had gotten out to wade along the reef again and I was with Joe in the skiff. He was poling near the edge of a flat when he sighted a school of bonefish patrolling back and forth in a deep cut off the flat's edge. The school seemed to follow a regular beat, moving first to one end of the cut then heading back toward the other end, and this made it possible to anticipate its movements and cast well ahead of the school. This also gave the lightly weighted Crazy Charlie time to sink to a level where the fish could see it when they arrived, and by fishing in this manner I hooked and landed two bonefish from the school, one a strong fish that ran twice into my backing.

Despite several disasters, my final count for the day was five bonefish hooked and four landed. Considering the hundreds of fish

we had seen, those were small numbers, but the fish had been decidedly less eager to take than the day before. Even so, it never seemed
as if the fishing was slow.

The following morning I was paired with George, a guide with
an uncanny ability to see fish. He quickly found a school of bones
tailing on a gorgeous flat next to an island he identified as Cutfinger
Caye. I hooked a fish immediately and for once everything went
right; after a spirited fight I gently released a handsome 3-pounder.

The fight had spooked the other fish in the school, however, so
we went looking elsewhere. George polled the skiff along Cutfinger
Caye's thick crop of mangroves and soon located several small
groups of bonefish cruising back among the tangled roots. I took fish
from two of these little schools, feeling lucky when they ran toward
open water after being hooked.

Then we sighted four fish cruising warily far back among the
roots in water so shallow it scarcely covered their backs. It was a difficult spot to get a fly into without hanging up on the mangrove roots,
and on my first several attempts the line fell over roots or leaves, but I
finally managed to drop the little Crazy Charlie in a narrow slot of
open water. The lead fish saw the fly, lunged forward, and took it
without hesitation. Like the others, it headed instantly for open water,
but this time the line whipped around a mangrove root. I thought
that would be the end of it, but the fish pulled so strongly that the
line slid up the root, over its top, and came free. I landed the fish after
a good fight and counted myself lucky again.

Later we moved to Calabash Flat, where Tommy and I had
fished the first day, and found bonefish tailing nearly everywhere, stir-
ring up huge "muds" over the flat. I cast into one of these and
watched the shadowy shape of a 5- or 6-pounder loom out of the
murk and swallow my fly. The fish ran hard, peeling off yards of

backing, and I held the curved rod high while the reel shrieked like a fat soprano. Backing whipped through the guides in a blur until the reel suddenly disgorged a backlash; a split second later the leader popped and the fish was gone. But in the next little while I landed six others, including one about 5-$\frac{1}{2}$ pounds, my best so far. The fish were again feeding with the same enthusiasm we had found on the first day.

Turneffe Island bonefish always have been known more for their numbers than for their average size, and that is still the case. We saw squads, platoons, companies, and whole regiments of bonefish—more than I'd ever seen in one place before. On some days we discovered huge schools feeding over the reef like cattle in a feedlot, on others they were rooting around on the flats like pigs after truffles. Most were less than 3 pounds, but there were enough 4- to 6-pounders to keep things interesting. Some larger fish also were seen, but none were hooked by members of our party.

The large schools were easy to locate and that usually made the fishing easy. Sometimes it was even possible to catch several fish from the same school before the rest spooked and ran away. The guides said it was unusual to find such large schools, speculating it might have been due to a succession of unusually high tides. Smaller schools and more fish traveling singly or in pairs are the norm at Turneffe Island, they said.

Most of the flats we fished were only a short distance from the lodge, which meant travel time was minimal, leaving more time to fish. The lodge's site, on the northeast shore of Little Caye Bokel, was once part of a single large island. Sometime after the lodge was built in the late 1950s, a storm cut through the island, leaving the lodge isolated on a 12-acre remnant since given its current name.

The lodge is a fully self-contained community, a cluster of buildings on stilts including a kitchen, staff quarters, engineering and carpenter shops, generator room, laundry, guest rooms, dive shop, compressor room, lounge, dining room, gift shop, and a small fishing shop. The Gay family had installed a new generator to provide a reliable source of electricity and a desalinization system to augment the supply of fresh water, formerly dependent on rainwater collected from the rooftops. The 12 guest rooms had been outfitted with air-conditioning units and new queen-size beds, and the bar had been remodeled and furnished with comfortable chairs, a large-screen television, videotape player, and stereo system. Electric wires had been buried to improve views, new skiffs and motors purchased, new quarters built for the guides and other staff members, and everything had a fresh coat of paint.

The lodge's 26-member staff was under the supervision of Warwick and Barbara Lowe, professional managers who made everything run like clockwork. The food was sensational; dinner entrées included coconut shrimp, lobster, filet mignon, stone crab, barbecued pork chops, and chicken. Breakfasts and lunches were equally large and tasty.

Bonefish are the most numerous species available at Turneffe Island, but permit also are plentiful, along with tarpon (in season), barracuda, and other species. After four days I'd caught enough bonefish to keep me happy for a while, so I decided to spend an afternoon fishing for permit, a new species for me. With Dale Spartas as my angling partner and Joe as our guide, we set out for a place called Nelson's Flat, reported to be a popular permit hangout.

When we got there we were treated to a strange scene. A Belizian native was standing in front of his beach hut using a palm switch to beat the rear end of a huge hog that was cooling itself in the shallow water near shore. The hog's owner wanted it to come ashore, while the hog understandably wanted to stay where it was.

The air was rent with porcine profanities while the owner beat the hog's ample rear end with the palm switch until the unfortunate beast finally gave up and reluctantly hauled itself out of the water like a beached submarine.

We were still chuckling over this when Joe whispered, "Permit!" We looked where he was pointing and saw the top half of a black sickle-shaped tail slicing through the waves. Beneath it was the oval shape of a large permit.

I told Dale to take the first shot and he climbed onto the bow platform and started casting, but the permit showed no interest in his fly. This was hardly surprising; permit are notoriously difficult to hook, and anglers have been known to chase them for years, even whole lifetimes, without ever connecting with one.

After the fish disappeared I traded places with Dale and waited on the casting platform while Joe poled across the flat.

"Permit," he said again. "See them?"

I looked and saw a school of three or four small permit cruising at an angle to the bow. Joe maneuvered skillfully to give me a better casting angle and I dropped the fly in front of the school, let it sink until the fish were nearly on top of it, then gave it a single quick twitch. The fish ignored it. I picked up the fly and repeated the process several times more, but the permit never showed the slightest interest. I continued casting with diminishing confidence as we followed the school until it finally got too far ahead of us and disappeared.

After that Joe staked out the skiff and we began wading the reef, looking for more permit. Soon we came upon two large ones, obviously feeding. By turns they would veer over the reef, then back into the slightly deeper water over the flats, then out over the reef again. Dale and I trailed on foot and cast to the fish as they crossed back and forth in front of us. One tailed for a long, breathtaking moment over Dale's fly without taking, then the other hovered over my crab pattern and gave it a long look before turning slowly away. We followed them at least 300 yards, making numerous presentations but receiving only those two heart-stopping looks, until finally the fish swam out of view.

"We find more of them," Joe said.

And we did. In three hours we saw 14 or 15 permit and cast to nearly all of them, but except for those two close encounters our offerings were greeted with total indifference. I spent only that single afternoon fishing for permit, but it was enough to gain an understanding of how some anglers become obsessed with the pursuit of this fascinating fish.

It was late in the season for tarpon, but we still made several morning or evening trips into the mangrove creeks to search for them. The morning expeditions meant the guides had to be up by 4 A.M., and often they were still hard at work after 6 P.M. Yet that was typical; I've never fished with a more friendly, knowledgeable, or hardworking set of guides. All were long-time Turneffe Island veterans, and they adapted readily to whatever schedule we wanted to keep.

Joe was my guide for three of the six days I fished. He was a happy, wiry little guy who hummed softly while he poled the boat, then mumbled to himself as he tried to figure out where fish might be. He was a fine fishing companion and I always felt comfortable in his capable hands.

One evening we searched for tarpon in a channel not far from the lodge, scouting the mangroves as the tide carried us along in the gathering twilight. Suddenly there was a sound like a pistol shot, which Joe said was a male dolphin slamming its tail against the water—a sign of mating activity. Soon we heard it again, then saw a pod of dolphins swimming toward us, breaching and blowing as they came. As they drew closer we could see the males alternately slamming their tails against the water and soaring above the waves in spectacular arcing leaps. We found no tarpon that evening, but the dolphin show made the trip worthwhile.

On our last morning Tommy Gay and I returned to Big Flat for a final try at bonefish or other targets of opportunity. The wind was stronger than it had been any other day that week, and the surf along the reef was high and roaring. Wading slowly, we encountered several single cruising bonefish and cast to each of them, but had only a single pull in response. Then we discovered a good-size school that appeared to be feeding, zigzagging over the reef in close formation as if guided by hidden signals. We followed, casting whenever we could get within range, and in the clear, shallow water over the reef we could see fish after fish change course and rush to inspect our flies, then turn away without taking. We started changing patterns after every few casts, hoping to find one that worked.

Finally a big bonefish charged forward and took my fly aggressively. The slack line was up instantly and through the guides, followed by the rest of the fly line and much of the backing. The fish ran far along the reef, a bright torpedo visible in the shallow surf, then suddenly veered toward blue water, ran the line around a chunk of coral, slipped the hook, and was gone.

It was the last fish I hooked at Turneffe Island, and I had lost it over the edge of the earth.

CHAPTER EIGHT

Salmon Brook Camp

Winter in Seattle. Gray sky, snow rotting on the ground like fungus on the back of a spawned-out salmon, wind from the north with the promise of more snow. Summer and New Brunswick seem far away, yet I know that when summer comes New Brunswick is where I will be.

I know also that somewhere, at this very moment, far out in the dark recesses of the North Atlantic, is a salmon I will catch. I do not know how old or how large it is, or even exactly what it looks like; I do not know if it is a buck or a hen, whether it is long and thin or short and full. I know nothing of the sights it has seen or the things it has experienced during the long instinctive journey from its native river out into the cold reaches of the Atlantic to feed and grow, or of the things it will experience on its return. I do not know when or exactly how I will catch it, yet somehow I know with certainty that I will. And on a cold January morning in Seattle, when summer and salmon rivers both seem very distant, that is a pleasant thing to contemplate.

For three years Howard Rossbach had invited me to fish with him at Salmon Brook Camp. The first two years I had said no, for reasons that seemed important at the time, but when he asked the third time there seemed no reason why I shouldn't go and many reasons why I should. So I said that I would, and in anticipation of the trip I wrote the words above on a winter morning, then promptly forgot them.

When the date for the trip finally rolled around, things got off to a highly unpromising start. Joan and I stepped off the airplane in Portland, Maine, only to discover the airline had lost the suitcase containing all our clothing. The next flight wasn't due until the following afternoon, so we had little choice except to wait in the hope it would have our suitcase aboard. As it happened, our suitcase was the very last off the plane, and we claimed it with vast relief and made a belated start for Bangor, where we were to meet our fishing companions— Howard, his wife, Katie, and Greg Hicks, another Seattle friend.

It was that evening in Bangor when I discovered my wallet was missing. A series of frantic telephone calls to places we had stopped brought the welcome news that the wallet had been found at the restaurant where we had eaten dinner. I drove back at desperate speed to reclaim it; fortunately, the contents—money, identification, credit cards—were intact.

After that it seemed nothing more could go wrong, and nothing did. We met Howard, Katie, and Greg the next morning and followed them on the freeway to the New Brunswick border, then east to Fredericton and north into the heart of the province. By early afternoon we were entering the village of Boiestown, where I had my first glimpse of the river I had come 3,000 miles to fish: the Main Southwest Miramichi.

The Miramichi has been called the greatest Atlantic salmon river in the world, and it certainly looked the part. It gleamed invitingly in the strong light of a late-June afternoon, a great wide swath of water sprawling comfortably in a shallow channel between hillsides clad with heavy growths of spruce, birch, pine, and rock maple.

But we had only a brief glimpse before the road turned away from the river and began climbing. The pavement narrowed, then

vanished altogether, and we found ourselves on a gravel road following a ridgetop covered with thick brush and tangled stands of second-
growth scrub. Occasional clearings revealed weather-battered homes
or cabins, but then even these disappeared and there was nothing but
impenetrable woods on either side of the narrowing road. Finally
Howard turned off on a narrow spur; we followed, shifting down to
lowest gear as the road dropped precipitously down the flank of the
ridge. Finally the road leveled out and emerged from the woods into a
large clearing dominated by a long, red-roofed building overlooking
the river; this was our destination, Salmon Brook Camp.

Howard had fished here since his teens, long before he moved
to the Pacific Northwest and we became friends, and it was his affec-
tionate talk of the place and its fishing that had persuaded us to
come. A small, private camp somewhat off the beaten track and limited to four rods, Salmon Brook is not as well known as many other
camps on the Main Southwest Miramichi, but to me that only made
it more attractive. Howard, Katie, Greg, and I would furnish the four
rods; we would fish while Joan relaxed, read, or hiked the trails
through the woods near camp.

The lodge itself was a long, narrow building, a single room
wide, with a covered veranda running its full length. The guest rooms
were at one end, with the kitchen, pantry, and guides' room at the
other, while a large main living and dining room occupied the
middle. The living room had paneled walls, a high beamed ceiling, a
handsome stone fireplace, fish carvings on the wall, and a small fly-
tying table in the corner. In every detail it fulfilled my expectations of
what a salmon camp should be.

The river flowed in a broad and shallow course past the camp,
with gentle open banks of water-silvered rock on either side. Winter-
pack ice scoured the banks annually, removing each summer's growth

of vegetation and leaving ample room for backcasts. Fishing from these banks would be easy.

Howard pointed out the mouth of a small brook on the far side of the river. This, he said, was Salmon Brook, the camp's namesake and primary reason for being. When the river's main stem warmed in summer, scores or sometimes even hundreds of salmon and grilse would congregate off the brook's mouth to seek the comfort of its cool, oxygenated water, he said, and these provided fair game for anglers from the camp. Even now, in late June, we could expect to find fresh spring-run salmon waiting off the brook.

Hearing that, we hastened to prepare for the evening fishing, rigging up rods, checking reels, lines, and leaders, and applying so many layers of insect repellent I felt I should prepare an environmental-impact statement. I had been advised the repellent was necessary to resist the attacks of bloodthirsty blackflies and no-see-ums, which had gathered around us from the moment we arrived. It was my first encounter with these pests and they turned out to be as vicious and persistent as everyone had warned me they would; fortunately, once we were surrounded by the chemical haze of the repellent, most of them remained at arm's length.

We rushed through supper without much thought for the food, then stepped outside to meet our guides. Howard introduced me to Charlie Munn, my guide for the week; he offered a strong, callused hand and his face showed the craggy, weathered look of many seasons on the river. In the traditional manner of salmon guides he seemed to speak only when spoken to, and then as sparingly as possible, but I managed to elicit from him the fact that he had guided at Salmon Brook for 26 years.

"Is there a rock in the river you don't know?" I asked.

"I guess not, I've hit 'em all," he replied.

We made our way down a steep flight of steps cut into the bank to a spot where four canoes were pulled up on the rocky shore. Charlie indicated which was his; I climbed into the bow and settled myself on the wooden seat. The canoe grated lightly on the rocks as he shoved off, hefted a spruce pole, and started poling us across the river. Up close, I could see the river's water was not as clear as it had seemed from a distance; it was red, almost the color of a Belgian ale.

We crossed the river quickly and Charlie guided the canoe expertly to shore between two rocks whose surfaces had been worn smooth by generations of anglers stepping out of canoes. We had drawn Murray's and Perley's Pools for the evening fishing, both directly across from camp. Murray's was a small drift, one that could be covered quickly and easily, but Perley's was a delightfully long and interesting pool. The tailout looked ideal for a riffle-hitched dry fly, the way I like to fish for steelhead on Northwest rivers, but here I was anxious to learn the approved local technique. Charlie recommended a deer hair fly fished on a floating line without a riffle hitch so the fly would ride in the surface film, and that was how I fished.

Casting from the beach, I covered both pools without result. Charlie then suggested we get in the canoe and fish the pools from their opposite sides, so I climbed in and he poled us to the center of the river, where he dropped a set of chains over the side to anchor the canoe. The fishing technique here was to cast from a sitting position in the bow of the canoe, starting with short casts, then lengthening them steadily until all the water within reach had been covered. Then Charlie would raise the anchor and allow the canoe to drop a short distance downstream, where we would repeat the whole business, and so on, until we had fully covered both pools. I had never before fished in this manner, but it was a comfortable way of fishing and I soon fell into the rhythm of it.

The evening was overcast and warm and the hours passed quickly. We saw two fish break, both beyond casting range, and nothing moved to my fly. It was nearly dark when the other canoes came into sight, bringing Howard, Katie, and Greg back from their own fishing, and Charlie hoisted the anchor and poled us back to camp. There Katie reported she had risen a fish that did not take. It was the only action any of us had experienced; nevertheless, I found myself looking forward to the next few days with optimism.

The next morning was overcast and cool, a fine morning for fishing. We headed downstream to our assigned pools—Betts Pool and the Grilse Hole. The ride was sweet and smooth, with the canoe slipping through the water like a hot knife through soft butter, and the only sounds were the gentle hiss of the river, the occasional crunch of Charlie's pole digging into gravel, and the far-off cry of jays in the woods.

Betts Pool and the Grilse Hole proved to be lovely stretches of water, each with long, enticing slicks marked by wrinkles and swirls revealing the presence of big boulders down below. We fished from the canoe, and although the water and conditions both seemed perfect, we saw no fish and I hooked nothing except a couple of small brook trout. When we returned to camp for lunch I learned the others had fared better: Katie had taken a handsome 4-pound grilse, Howard had risen and missed a fish, and Greg had caught a nice brook trout. My turn, it seemed, should be next.

It came that evening. The weather was still cloudy when we started out, but the clouds soon dissolved into a clear, light blue twilight sky with a cold-looking gibbous moon. We had drawn the pool at the mouth of Salmon Brook, a stretch only about 25 yards long but perhaps twice as wide, with a good possibility of finding salmon or grilse in every inch of it. Since the pool was short and did not take long to fish, Charlie explained the usual method was to fish it first from shore, then change fly patterns and fish it again, and if several passes with different patterns yielded nothing we would get in the canoe, anchor out in the river, and fish the outside edge of the pool.

Following his instructions, I made two trips through the pool without result, using different flies each time, then changed again and started a third pass. This time I had a long, slow take from a heavy fish that began running downstream immediately, found a rock and took my line around it, then headed upstream again and jumped twice, high and handsome—a beautiful salmon of 10 or 12 pounds, thick and deep, its gunmetal colors flashing in the twilight. After the second jump it headed downstream once again, unwittingly freeing my line from the rock and restoring a tight connection. It ran farther and I followed while Charlie kept pace, landing net at the ready, shouting encouragement.

The fish took all my line and a long length of backing in a noisy, angry run, then turned suddenly and came in close to shore, holding in a deep slot while I recovered most of the line I had lost. Then it leaped again, twice, shaking itself like a wet puppy and throwing spray each time, but the hook still held. Changing tactics, the fish moved back out into deeper water, where it settled down and began to sulk. Putting on all the strain I dared, I got it moving again and the fish followed grudgingly as I led it near shore. For a moment it was almost within arm's reach, the leader butt showing above the surface, but then it began slowly edging away, back toward the center of the river. Suddenly it leaped again, coming straight up out of the water like a missile, and it was still hanging in midair when I saw the fly come away.

Charlie, standing next to me, saw it too. "Saved you the trouble of releasing it," he said, trying to make me feel better. "You had your fun with it."

I supposed he was right; the battle had been great fun. But since it was the first real sea-run Atlantic salmon I'd ever hooked, I couldn't help wishing the fight had gone the other way.

Later we fished the outer edge of the pool from the canoe and I had another take—a swirl on the surface followed by a brief, hard pull—but the fish was not hooked. Since I had momentarily felt its weight and the fish almost certainly had felt the hook, Charlie was of the opinion it wouldn't come again, but we tried for it anyway; I changed flies three times and hammered the spot until it was obvious Charlie was right. Still, we saw four or five other fish jump in the pool, indicating there were plenty of salmon in the river, and I took that as a sign of encouragement for the days ahead.

The following day was Monday and while other people all over the world were going to work, the four of us went fishing. As if in celebration of our freedom, the sun rose over the northern hills and flooded the river with light, and soon the Miramichi was fairly bursting with hatching flies and the rises of hungry salmon parr and brook trout. Charlie poled us across and upstream to Black Rock Pool, just below the Brook Pool, where we would start fishing.

Black Rock yielded nothing and I had just started fishing Baker Pool, the next downstream, when I had a soft take from a fish that soon ran strongly. Taking line in noisy gulps, it led me on a chase all the way down through the pool below, then paused and jumped three times. These efforts seemed to take the edge from its strength, for it then settled down and fought stubbornly in deeper water. Eventually I gained the advantage and managed to steer the fish close to the beach where Charlie was waiting with his long-handled net; with a deft stab he had the fish in its mesh. Hoisting the writhing salmon into the air, he read the scale in the net handle and announced the fish's weight at 9 pounds—9 graceful pounds of wild silver-gray beauty. A hen fish, it had taken the same Green Machine fly pattern I had used to hook the fish I'd lost the night before.

Charlie quickly backed the hook out of the salmon's jaw and resuscitated it in the river, then finally let it go. The fish swam away slowly, its bright sides flashing like a signal mirror until it was swallowed up in the red-stained depths. I watched it go, wondering which of us had come farther to the river.

That was my only fish of the morning, but Greg landed a fine 13-pounder after a long fight and Howard lost another salmon at the beach, so we had much to talk about at lunch.

Later that afternoon we drove downriver to the sleepy hamlet of Doaktown. The place seemed almost uninhabited until we entered the refurbished old house that was headquarters for the famous W. W. Doak fly shop; inside the place was jammed with people. It seemed as if all of them were talking at once and all the talk was of salmon. I moved through the crowd and listened to the conversation as I inspected the displays of fine rods, reels, waders, books, angling accessories, and hundreds of flies housed neatly in compartmented trays. It was the kind of shop I love, filled with the ambience of fish and fishermen, and an hour later, when I left, my arms were burdened with packages—souvenir shirts, a new fly box stocked with some of Doak's best patterns, and other odds and ends. A visit to Doak's is a pilgrimage every Miramichi angler ought to make.

By the time we returned to camp the weather was changing and the ribbon of sky visible over the river was growing dark with rain-fat clouds. The river seemed ominously quiet as Charlie poled us downstream to Betts Pool and the Grilse Hole, which we had drawn again for the evening fishing.

But it did not remain quiet long, for I soon struck two fish in the Grilse Hole. The first was a grilse that chased the fly far across the surface and finally seized it with a hard pull, yet somehow escaped without being hooked and refused to come again. The second also was a grilse that I covered after seeing it rise twice; this one took the fly firmly and Charlie quickly put me ashore to play it. It fought it in a series of short, strong runs, finally tiring, until I was able to bring it almost within range of Charlie's long-handled net. Then the hook suddenly pulled out.

After that we kept fishing until the river was only a silver reflection of the darkening sky. I settled back in the bow seat and watched for the distant lights of camp to come into view as Charlie poled us back upstream against the shallow flow of the river.

Few rivers dominate their physical or social surroundings as much as the Miramichi. Rising in the western central highlands of New Brunswick, its numerous sources include tamarack bogs, which give the river its distinctive red color. It flows generally eastward, collecting runoff from countless tributaries draining the whole midsection of the province. Like Salmon Brook, many of its tributaries are small, while others—such as the Cains and the Northwest Miramichi—are full-fledged rivers in their own right. The channel of the Main Southwest broadens to accommodate this ever-increasing volume of water, helped by the annual scouring of winter-pack ice that widens the channel even more. Flowing over hard bedrock, the river remains shallow until it reaches the upper limit of the tide from the Gulf of Saint Lawrence.

The Indians who first inhabited this land relied on the river's salmon for food and used the river itself for transportation. These same attributes, along with the lure of timber, attracted the first white settlers to the Miramichi country. The river's lower valley was first settled by Acadians, but they were later evicted by the British, who then occupied the land themselves. They tapped the salmon runs and cut the best timber to make masts for their sailing ships, and their flourishing industries brought a period of prosperity to the region that continued late into the 19th century. By then, however, the age of wooden ships had passed, much of the virgin timber was gone, and the salmon runs had suffered greatly from commercial fishing and the harsh environmental impacts of logging. With its natural resources all but used up, New Brunswick entered a period of economic eclipse from which it still has not fully recovered.

To the extent that any recovery has taken place, much of it again has been due to the Miramichi. Belatedly recognizing the economic worth of the salmon sport fishery, the province now manages the river for sportfishing, with regulations designed to assure preservation of its salmon runs. Meanwhile, a federal buyout program has ended the commercial net fishery, allowing more and larger salmon to return to the river and further increasing its value to anglers. Now public and private fishing camps employ hundreds, perhaps thousands, of New Brunswick citizens, and the many businesses supporting these camps provide even more jobs. Once again the river is providing livelihoods for the people who live along its banks, and the Miramichi today is one of New Brunswick's most important economic assets. The story of its success surely offers a lesson for other provinces and states.

The Miramichi is such a long and complex river system that it would be impossible for one person to learn every pool and run throughout its length. That would be true even if there was not so much to learn, because many of the river's best reaches are privately owned or leased and access is available only at a price, if at all. Gary Anderson, in his fine book *Atlantic Salmon & the Fly Fisherman*, summed up the complexity of the river's ownership:

> Things are most entangled where settlement has
> had the longest history and fathers have divided their
> land among their sons, who in turn have encouraged

their children to build on a plot near home. In this way the shoreline has been divided and subdivided, with the result that some fishing rights are owned by someone other than the landowner, having been sold off at some previous time. Thus a natural pool may be divided into sections with different owners. In some cases one is permitted to fish perhaps a hundred meters of public shoreline, only to be obliged to stop fishing at an arbitrary boundary signifying privately owned water. . . . Opposite shores often have different owners, each entitled to fish to the center of the river. In some narrow pools, or in periods of low water, this means that two owners can sometimes cast over the same fish from opposite shores.

As the river changes from year to year, and boundary lines are seldom well surveyed or marked, disputes sometimes arise between neighbors, particularly as the fishing is always somehow better on the other side of the line. Fortunately, the province has purchased and continues to purchase angling rights, and has made (some of) the water accessible to the public. . . . It must be acknowledged, however, that even in the headwaters, prime pools of the Main Southwest Miramichi tend to be in private hands.

All of which is yet another good reason to patronize one of the river's many camps, where the problem of ownership and access may be safely left in the hands of camp operators and guides.

Salmon Brook Camp, built in 1929 for a group of Pennsylvania and New York anglers, is among the oldest private camps on the Main Southwest Miramichi. The original lodge building burned in 1964, but the existing structure was built to the same design. The camp is still owned by a small group of private shareholders, but to generate the income necessary to keep it self-sustaining the camp is rented out to nonshareholders for many weeks of the season. This means you don't have to be a shareholder to fish at Salmon Brook, although it helps to know a shareholder, or to know someone who does—like Howard.

Eight pools are fished from the camp, including the Brook Pool (at the mouth of Salmon Brook), Black Rock, Baker, Murray's, Perley's, Stickney's, Betts, and the Grilse Hole. At least they are called pools, although most are not really pools in the classic sense; in the parlance of steelhead anglers they would probably be called runs, for most are short stretches of fairly fast water with good depth and scattered boulders offering places for migrating fish to rest. Except for Perley's and Stickney's (the latter fished only from a canoe at high water), all are small enough that a good caster can cover them easily in a short time, and once he has done that there's nothing left to do but change flies and cover them again. This can get monotonous, especially when the fish are not taking well, but when the salmon are "traveling," as they often are, there is always a chance a fish will come into a pool even after the first or second time you've fished it. So it makes sense to go through each pool again and again.

The period we had chosen to fish—the last week in June—is not among the most popular weeks of the season, because the numbers of fish are not as great as they will be later; the numbers of blackflies, on the other hand, may be at their peak. But the late-June fish—the so-called spring "bluebacks"—have a reputation for being "hot" fish with more spirit and energy than those taken later in the season, after the water has warmed.

Like most fishing camps, Salmon Brook maintains a catch register. Its entries begin in 1936 and in all the time since there are only a few entries for the month of June. The entries are sparse in any case, usually giving only numbers of salmon and grilse caught, the weight of the fish, the date, name of pool, fly pattern, and angler's name—and sometimes not even that much. Some entries have a few added comments about the weather or the river conditions, and some are weighted with the kind of inane remarks that people seem compelled to write in such journals.

Not surprisingly, the record shows that grilse have nearly always outnumbered salmon in the catch, and during those long, dark years when few returning salmon escaped the commercial nets, the record leans even more heavily toward grilse; a salmon of double-digit weight was rare indeed during those times. But a joyful notation appears at the head of the 1972 record—"First year that commercial fishing was banned!"—and that season's salmon catch was dramatically larger than it had been in previous years. The salmon catch has remained consistently larger ever since, with the number of salmon occasionally even surpassing the number of grilse taken annually in the camp waters.

The largest fish noted in the register was a 46-inch salmon weighing more than 38 pounds, caught in Stickney's Pool August 15, 1990, during a period of extremely high water. Over the 60-year span of the record, only six other salmon of 30 pounds or more have been recorded, and all those were caught within the past ten years—further proof of the salutary effect of the end of commercial netting.

A 30-pound salmon was the last thing on my mind when I awoke the next morning to a dark, gray dawn. The rain started just as we headed out for the morning fishing and soon came in torrents, driven by a cold wind that dashed heavy drops into our faces. The river looked sullen under rain, and so it proved to be; I fished Murray's and Perley's Pools, covering each thoroughly, but saw no sign of fish. Even the guides seemed less attentive to their chores, huddling together in olive-drab rain gear, barely visible through the sheets of rain.

After the morning's fishing we dried off back at the lodge and gathered for lunch in the dining room, while the guides did the same in their own room. This separation between anglers and guides struck me as a curious thing, almost like the enforced distance between officers and enlisted men in the armed forces. Only on the river were we ever close to the guides; at other times there was little or no contact.

The arm's-length relationship made me feel a little uncomfortable; I would like to have known these men better, to have heard more of their stories, shared their humor, perhaps learned some of the secrets they had gleaned from years on the river. But that is not considered acceptable form; in fact, the separation between anglers and guides is traditional and long standing, and there are reasons why this is so. One, I was told, is that alcoholism is common among Miramichi guides, as it is among fishing guides nearly everywhere, so it is thought best to keep the guides away from their "sports" during off-duty hours—especially since some of the sports might be expected to contribute to the problem. Abuse of alcohol did not appear to be a problem for any of the guides at Salmon Brook, but we still carefully observed the tradition; they kept to themselves off the river, and so did we.

That afternoon the rain continued, finally subsiding to a misty drizzle by the time we were ready for the evening fishing. The air was moist and cool, the trees along the river crouched under the weight of rain clinging to their leaves, and the river itself had risen slightly, covering some of the smaller rocks along the shore. Charlie greeted me with the unwelcome observation that the salmon "don't take so good" when the river is rising.

As usual, he was right. I fished Black Rock Pool twice and Baker three times, changing flies each time, without so much as a touch. Howard, Greg, and Katie also drew blanks.

More rain fell that night and the river rose several inches more, its color darkening from red to rust and its temperature falling from 65 to 60, then even lower. That was more bad news, Charlie said; Miramichi salmon take best when the temperature is above 65 and seldom respond to a fly when it drops below, he explained. That surprised me until I thought about it; temperatures above 65 are considered high on most rivers, but the Miramichi is shallow with dark water that warms quickly, and its salmon undoubtedly have adapted to this, remaining active at temperatures that would approach lethality for fish in other rivers.

That realization didn't make me feel any better about our prospects; it only meant that Charlie was probably right again. The next three days proved the point; during that period I took only one grilse, had another fish on for two clicks of the reel, and missed a third that rose to my fly. Howard also caught two grilse, but those were the only fish we saw during that time.

On our last day the rain finally stopped and Charlie and I made a final trip to Betts Pool and the Grilse Hole on a warm, clear evening. The moon, which had been invisible for several nights, was now almost full, and its light cast a long reflected path on the water as we headed downstream. Neither of us said much as I fished in the golden light of the quiet evening. At the head of Betts Pool I rose and briefly touched a grilse but failed to hook it, and that was all.

When it was time to head back, I settled one last time on the wooden seat in the bow of Charlie's canoe and listened again to the rhythmic crunch of his pole digging into the river-bottom gravel and the hiss of water sliding past the hull. Full darkness had fallen by the time we reached camp, but fireflies were winking on and off in the grass in front of the lodge and the air was balmy. It was a lovely night in a lovely place.

The week had passed all too quickly—so quickly it left me wondering how six days of fishing could pass in only four. I had risen eight fish, hooked four, and landed a single salmon and a single grilse—and felt certain the total would have been higher had it not been for the several days of rain. But bad weather is a risk you take no matter where or when you fish, and rain or no rain, I was well satisfied and happy for the chance to visit this fascinating land of blackflies and bright salmon.

Back home, many months later, I came across those words of anticipation I had written on that snowy January morning. Their prophecy had been fulfilled.

PART III

Things

CHAPTER NINE

Blue Heaven

Mayflies and I go back a long way together. I suppose the first one I ever saw was on the little neighborhood stream where I fished as a boy, long before I was old enough even to know what mayflies were. It wasn't until a few years later, when I began reading fishing books, that I found out.

Some books I read described mayflies in dry technical language, but most treated them in personal or anecdotal terms. Other insect hatches—stoneflies, caddisflies, midges, and so on—were covered in ordinary fashion, but when the subject got around to mayflies the writers usually started using words that evoked a scarcely suppressed feeling of excitement, which easily communicated itself to me. It was, I suppose, similar to the excitement a trout must feel when mayflies begin hatching.

The more I read about mayflies, the more I began to appreciate their importance. Perhaps more fly patterns have been designed to imitate mayflies than any other insect—maybe even *all* other insects; moreover, the whole sport of fly fishing seems to have evolved from efforts to imitate the mayfly. It is probably no exaggeration to say that fly fishing as we know it would not exist if the mayfly hadn't been there to give it inspiration.

Understanding their importance made me pay close attention to the drawings and photographs of mayflies in my books and try to memorize enough of their details so I could be certain of recognizing the genuine article if I should encounter it on the waters I fished.

Once I had a good idea of what to look for, it wasn't long before I found it.

One of the first times was a cloudy, dark day early in a new trout season. I was fishing a shallow, weedy bay in a lowland lake known for its large rainbow trout. The water was placid as I steered my little rowboat into the bay, and at first I saw no sign of feeding trout. Then I noticed a sudden subtle crease in the surface as a trout made a pass at something I could not see; soon came another, and within moments there were many more. Small, dark, blue-gray flies began popping magically to the surface in growing numbers, and it was obvious these were the objects of the trout's interest. Looking closely at one of them, I was thrilled to see it looked just like the pictures in all my books; it was a mayfly beyond doubt, and my own excitement rose to match the feverish mood of the trout.

I had no fly that was a close imitation of the natural, so I chose the next best thing I had—an ordinary Gray Hackle Peacock that was close in size if not in form or color. It didn't matter to the trout; all their normal caution was forgotten in a frenzy to capture the fat little flies that were now hatching all over the surface of the bay, and they seized my clumsy fly with the same fervor they displayed for the naturals. In my nervous excitement I struck too hard and broke off the first two or three fish that took my fly. After that I called a mental time-out and made a conscious effort to calm down.

When I felt ready I resumed casting, and when the next rise came I set the hook more gently, hooked the trout solidly, and landed it after a brisk fight. Others soon followed, seven in all before the hatch petered out and the bay again became still; the smallest weighed nearly 2 pounds and the largest was well above 3. It was one of the best fishing days I'd had up to that time, and although it was many years ago, the experience remains as vivid as if it had happened yesterday.

Looking back on it now, I also realize it marked an important milestone in my fly-fishing life: Until then I had been a confirmed wet-fly fisherman, but after that the dry fly became my method of choice.

Since then I've seen mayflies hatch on many waters and in many sizes and colors—from the tiny, almost invisible, black-and-white *Tricorythodes*, whose prolific numbers coat the surfaces of some rivers like dust, to the large, yellow-green giant *Hexagenia*, or green drake, a mighty mouthful for any trout. I've seen them at almost every season of the year, on great rivers and small brooks, on windswept lakes and in the dark waters of little beaver ponds. My fly boxes now are filled with a great assortment of imitations in all colors and sizes, and I have caught fish on nearly every one of them. But of all the mayflies I have encountered in a long fishing life, there is one I treasure above all others: the spinner stage of the *Callibaetis*, otherwise known as the Blue Upright.

Callibaetis is the great stillwater mayfly of the American West, common in the many high-desert and semi-alpine lakes that sprawl eastward from the spine of the Cascades all the way from northern California to southern British Columbia. It is present in many shallow, rich coastal lowland lakes as well. Most entomologists agree the genus includes at least 23 species, of which as many as 14 or 15 are found in the Far West. Fortunately, they are all similar enough in appearance that a good imitation of one usually will serve as an imitation for most of the others; that makes life much easier for fly fishers.

Anglers know these flies by many local names—Speckle-winged Spinners, Bandwings, or Cream Hen Spinners, to mention just a few—but I have always known the spinner stage as the Blue Upright, or Blue for short, because it was introduced to me by that name. There are other mayflies with more colorful or romantic names—the Pale Morning Dun and Blue-Winged Olive come readily to mind—but none, I think, has a name more perfectly suited to its appearance or behavior.

Blue is the color of the adult spinner's body, actually dark navy blue, almost black, but it could just as easily stand for blue blood, for to me the *Callibaetis* is the royalty of mayflies. Upright is an apt description of the posture of the newly emerged spinner—always poised, cocky, and erect—but it might apply equally to its behavior, for the Blue Upright is always well mannered, a benign, gentle creature that sacrifices itself readily to satisfy the appetites of hungry trout and the anxious hopes of trout fishermen.

One of many things I like about the Blue Upright is its punctuality. On late-June days, when the sky is clear and the sun is bright, the *Callibaetis* spinners begin to appear magically at the stroke of noon. One moment the air is empty and quiet; then suddenly they are there, all around you, bobbing and weaving gracefully, rising and falling, resting on your collar, sleeves, or hat, falling into the water, vanishing into the mouths of hungry trout.

Or hungry salmon. For the Blue Upright spinner fall is one of the most important fishing events at Hosmer Lake in Oregon, long the home of transplanted Atlantic salmon. There, precisely at noon on most warm June days, spinners emerge from the sedge grass around the shoreline and fly over the lake to lay their eggs, then fall spent to the surface.

A generation ago, when I began fishing the lake, it held transplanted sea-run Atlantic salmon of large size, and these fish were well acquainted with the habits of the spinners. They would cruise the shoreline, sometimes in water only inches deep, waiting for the egg-laying flights to begin and the spinners to start falling. A tiny Blue Upright imitation cast in front of one of these cruising fish always brought a close look, often a bold rise.

That would have been exciting in itself, but the fishing had an extraordinary visual quality that made it even more spectacular: It was possible to see a fish approaching from a long distance, cast well ahead of it, then watch as it drew near, caught sight of the fly, rushed forward, tilted up to inspect it closely—and then sometimes sucked it in. It was hard to believe such large fish could be interested in such small flies, but thankfully they were, and when hooked they nearly always treated the angler to an unforgettable performance—a series of incredible leaps or screaming, high-speed runs across the lake's shallow flats.

I had many wonderful days fishing Blue Upright spinner falls on Hosmer Lake, but the best was the day I landed the two largest salmon I ever caught there. They came one after the other, each rising delicately to inhale a size 16 Blue Upright, each putting up a spectacular fight with many long runs and several jumps before coming finally to the net. I weighed each fish in the net before releasing it; the first pulled the scale down to the 7-pound mark and the second registered exactly one pound heavier.

Those big salmon are long gone now, victims of both natural circumstances and management neglect. They have been replaced by true landlocked salmon from Maine that do not grow as large, rise as willingly, or fight as well. But the Blue Uprights are still there, and they still swarm around the margins of the lake on warm June afternoons, sometimes enticing even the dour landlocks to rise. When that happens, a little Blue Upright imitation still takes its share of fish.

The life cycle of the *Callibaetis* is similar to that of most mayflies. A tiny nymph hatches from the egg and begins life in the tangled stems of underwater plants or bottom debris near the shores of lakes or ponds. The nymph goes through a succession of molts as it grows larger, shedding its old skin each time. After the final molt, when the nymph is mature, it ascends to the surface, splits open, and the first winged adult stage—the dun, or subimago—emerges from the nymphal shuck. The dun flies to the nearest land and takes shelter in foliage, waiting for yet another molt, which produces the second winged stage—the spinner, or imago. The spinners then mate and the females fly over the surface of the lake to lay their eggs, which hatch almost as soon as they enter the water, and the insect's life cycle is complete. The spinner stage arguably produces the best fly fishing, but nymphs and duns also are taken avidly by trout, which makes them of nearly equal interest to fly fishers.

It is easy to recognize the nymphs. They are larger than most mayfly nymphs and the majority of *Callibaetis* species have three tails, while most other mayfly nymphs have only two. Grayish brown in color, the nymphs also have rows of distinctive heart-shaped gills along either side of their abdomens. When active, they move about in short, rapid bursts, propelled by quick thrusts of their abdomens and tails. They eat algae and microscopic diatoms and play a major role in converting vegetable matter to animal tissue in lakes; one researcher has called them "the cattle or rabbits" of stillwater aquatic environments.

The nymphs are easy targets for a host of aquatic predators, and many do not survive to maturity. Those able to avoid being eaten may reach maturity in as little as six weeks after hatching, although it takes longer in most aquatic environments. The fully developed nymph has a prominent pair of dark wing pads on its back and begins moving about restlessly, swimming toward the surface as if in rehearsal for hatching, then returning to rest again on the stems of underwater plants. Often this behavior sets off a frenzied spell of feeding by trout, further reducing the number of nymphs available for hatching.

Finally, in obedience to instinct, the nymph makes a last ascent all the way to the surface film, and the transformation that then takes place is one of the most remarkable in all of nature: The skin of the nymph splits open down the back and an entirely different creature, the dun, emerges. Slim and graceful in shape, it bears little resemblance to the blunt, stubby nymph from which it came. It also has wings, which the nymph lacks altogether, and these are tall and triangular in shape, giving the fly a distinctive profile on the water. The dun has only two tails instead of three, as on most of the nymphs, and its whole body, from the forelegs to the tips of its tails, is a sort of dull Confederate gray in color.

After hatching, the dun abandons its nymphal shuck like an empty life raft and floats on the surface waiting for its newly unfolded wings to dry. At this juncture it is at the mercy of the wind, which may carry it long distances across the surface; it is also totally exposed and vulnerable to capture by feeding trout and birds. The few moments it takes for the wings to dry are among the most perilous of the mayfly's existence, and many duns end up in the stomachs of predators. As soon as their wings are dry, the survivors rise from the surface in graceful flight and head for shore.

The duns often hatch on cold, wet, blustery days, frequently after squalls of rain or snow, and this adds to their peril; it takes longer for their wings to dry in such weather, so their exposure to feeding trout and birds is even greater than it might be otherwise.

In warmer coastal lowland lakes, hatches may begin as early as late February and continue sporadically all through the summer into late fall. The high-desert lakes have shorter seasons; many remain frozen until mid-May, so the first duns ordinarily do not appear until the end of May or the first weeks of June, and the hatches usually end by mid-September.

While never as prolific as the spinner flights, dun hatches still provide exciting angling opportunities. Often the onset of a hatch is signaled by the swirls of trout feeding under water on nymphs ascending to the surface; then the first duns appear on the surface and the trout come slashing after them, rising and plunging and feeding eagerly. But it is never a case of all one or all the other; even while some trout are busily rising to duns, others continue to feed eagerly on nymphs beneath the surface. This presents anglers with the dilemma of whether to fish an imitation of the nymph or the dun. For me, ever since that long-ago day when I took those seven heavy rainbows, the answer has always been clear: If there is any chance at all of taking fish on a floating fly I would rather do it that way than any other, even if it might mean catching fewer fish.

Curiously, the emerging duns always seem too few in number to account for the vast swarms of spinners that later appear in the mating flights. There are a couple of reasons for this. One is that many dun hatches take place in late evening or at night, when anglers do not see them; the other is that while duns make their final molt into spinners within a day of hatching, they may then wait several days for warmer weather before they start their mating flights, and by then their cumulative numbers are great.

The transformation that takes place when the dun molts and becomes a spinner is almost as remarkable as the change from the nymph to the dun. The prominent gray wings of the dun are replaced by a smaller pair of shiny, glasslike wings, transparent except for a gridlike network of dark mottled veins along their leading edges. These dark veins are responsible for the name Speckle-winged Spinner, by which these flies are known in some quarters. The gray body of the dun yields to the dark navy blue or black of the spinner, which also has thin gold bands separating each body segment. This color scheme covers the upper two-thirds of the spinner's body, while the lower third, or belly, is a creamy brown, almost buckskin color. The eyes of the spinner, always much larger in males than females, are brown and prominent, and its twin tails are a light, smoky blue. In overall size the spinner is smaller than the dun and much more delicate and fragile in appearance. Fresh from its final molt, with wings cocked erect and forelegs held high, the spinner is the very image of its name, the Blue Upright.

The spinners do not feed; at this stage of their lives they are occupied solely with mating and depositing their eggs. Their mating flights are a thing of beauty; the air is filled with countless flies, dancing up and down with apparently limitless energy as if powered by the sun. From a distance one of these mating swarms may look like a column of dark smoke; up close it resembles nothing so much as a shower of sparks rising from a campfire.

The male spinners fly rhythmically up and down, while the females dart horizontally through the swarm. Males seize the females from below and copulation takes place in flight. Once their mating is complete, the females return to the shelter of foliage along the shore to rest and wait for their eggs to develop. Then, when the next warm day comes, they make their final flights and lay their eggs.

The first flies usually appear at noon and are soon joined by others, then many more, until by 2 P.M. they are everywhere. They drop to the surface again and again, shedding a portion of their cargo of tiny eggs each time, until the eggs are gone and their strength is nearly spent. Then they fall to the surface one last time and settle there, unable to rise again.

For a while their tiny transparent wings remain erect and poised, but soon enough they lose even the strength necessary to hold them up; the shining wings begin to droop, opening slowly to a 45-degree angle, then to a wider angle still, until at last the spinner lies spread-eagled on the surface, fully spent.

By 3 P.M. the egg-laying flight is over; the air is empty, but the lake's surface is littered with the wreckage of thousands of spent flies. Even in this condition the spinners remain prime targets for hungry trout, and because there are so many of them they trigger some of the most incredible rises an angler can ever hope to see. This is what makes the blue upright spinner fall such a productive time to fish.

The heaviest spinner falls take place in June on most waters I fish, and I suspect the same is true for the majority of lakes and ponds throughout the western range of the *Callibaetis*. But other falls come later in the season, for in most circumstances the *Callibaetis* produces several generations a year. I have fished spinner falls on high-elevation lakes in British Columbia as late as mid-September, normally a time when most anglers have given up any hope of taking fish on dry flies. A curious thing about the *Callibaetis* is that when multiple generations occur in a single season, the adult flies of each new generation will be smaller than those of the one before, which means anglers may need smaller imitations for September fishing than for May or June.

Many fly patterns have been devised to imitate the different stages in the life cycle of the *Callibaetis*. A small Gold-Ribbed Hare's Ear Nymph makes a passable imitation of the nymph, although just about any dubbed gray or gray-brown pattern of appropriate size will do. Dun and spinner imitations usually must be more exact, for trout seem more discriminating about flies on the surface than those underneath. For many years I have enjoyed success imitating both spinners and duns with variations of a pattern acquired originally from Dick Alf of Sun Valley. It's called the Hatchmatcher or Hatchmaster.

The Hatchmatcher is really more a generic style of tying than a specific pattern. The dressing requires only two feathers—one for the tail, body, and wing of the mayfly, the other to provide a few turns of hackle.

A natural or dyed mallard breast feather is most often used for the tail, body, and wing. The fibers of this feather are reversed and compressed (leaving some at the feather's tip to serve as the tail of the fly), then secured to the hook shank so that the rear portion of the feather forms the body and the front fibers form the wing, which is fastened in an upright position with figure-eight windings. After that the tip of the mallard breast feather is trimmed away so that only a single fiber remains on either side of the quill; these fibers stick out in a V-shape, imitating the twin tails of a real mayfly. A few turns of hackle from the second feather are added, and the fly is complete.

That's the generic dressing, which can be used to imitate any adult mayfly. Simple to tie and highly durable, it makes a deadly imitation of either dun or spinner, depending on the colors used. Yet despite its many virtues, to my knowledge the details of this pattern have been given in only two books, my own *Kamloops* and *Flies of the Northwest*, compiled by the Inland Empire Fly Fishing Club of Spokane (both from Frank Amato Publications, Portland, Oregon).

Other feathers may be substituted for mallard breast, and I have found that a shiny metallic green feather from the neck of a wild Chinese pheasant rooster usually works best to imitate the body and wing of the Blue Upright spinner. The pheasant feather has stiffer fibers and requires more "persuasion" to form into the shape of the spinner's body, but in the process of stroking and compression these fibers lose their metallic luster and become a dark blue-gray color, closely matching the upper body of the natural. The quill of the pheasant neck feather also is a dark creamy brown, which closely matches the belly of a real spinner. When tied on a size 16 hook, with a few turns of natural black hackle on either side of the wing, this combination makes a superb imitation of the Blue Upright. A spent-wing version, tied without any hackle, also works well during the latter stages of a spinner fall.

I use a dark gray goose flank feather for the body, wing, and tail of the *Callibaetis* dun; when this feather is shaped properly and a few turns of natural black hackle are added, the result is a dark pattern that imitates the dun very closely. I tie this pattern on size 12 or 14 hooks.

Like the naturals they are intended to imitate, these patterns are extremely fragile in appearance, but they hold up amazingly well and float without the need for any dry-fly dressing. On occasion I have taken more than 20 fish on the same fly before it became so torn and tattered I was forced to change. I keep my fly boxes stocked with many more spinner patterns than duns, reflecting the more common occurrence and greater profligacy of spinner falls compared to dun emergences on most of the waters I fish.

There are, of course, many other prolific and important hatches on western lakes. The great traveling sedge hatches of the Kamloops trout lakes of British Columbia are in a class by themselves, and the rare spring and fall flights of winged ants that take place on some western waters can produce dry-fly fishing of a kind rarely equaled. But if ever a kind Providence created a single fly expressly for the purpose of closing the enchanted circle that begins with a hungry trout and ends with a satisfied angler, the *Callibaetis* is that fly. At every stage of its life it offers food for trout and opportunities for anglers.

But I love the final stage best, the stage of the spinner or Blue Upright. I love watching them settle in upside-down rows along the brim of my old, sweat-stained fishing hat, their clear glassy wings folded neatly and their long smoky blue tails waving gently in the breeze. I love seeing them land softly on the lenses of my sunglasses, so close my eyes cannot focus on them and I can see them only as blue-black smudges against a distant sky. I love watching their quick graceful movements as they dance in the air around me, and I love the feel of their dainty, soft-as-breath touch against my skin.

They are as fragile as old lace, as delicate as if made of some gossamer substance plucked from the wind, the kindest and most gentle of insects. In endless numbers they swarm and sway in blue blizzards over western lakes, glittering in the afternoon sunlight like magic dust from a Disney movie, then falling like dark raindrops to the surface where trout come for them in eager slashing rises. To be on the water then, to be among the falling spinners and the feeding trout, to cast a tiny Blue Upright imitation into the maelstrom of rises, is to experience the very essence of fly fishing at its best.

That's as good as it gets. That's Blue Heaven.

CHAPTER TEN

Raising Cane

Rods, reels, fly boxes, nets, creels, vests—these and the countless other things fly fishers use are among the great fascinations of the sport. For some anglers, making or owning them becomes as important as fishing itself.

Letcher Lambuth was one who felt that way. His greatest satisfaction came from making his own fly-fishing tackle, and though he is now best remembered for his bamboo fly rods, he also made nearly everything else he used for fishing.

None of the things he made was ordinary. He was one of only two bamboo rod builders ever to make spiral rods (the other was Fred Divine of Utica, New York). Creating his own designs and inventing his own tools, Letcher built hexagonal (six-sided) rods that were twisted one-sixth of a turn between guides, so that each guide rested on a different face, or spline, of the rod. This, he believed, gave his rods greater strength and smoother action than conventional bamboo rods with straight sections. Those who used his rods agreed.

Letcher also designed, cut, and sewed his own fishing vest, one of the first ever made. He learned to crochet so he could make a fishing creel of cotton twist with spaces between the fibers that would allow air to circulate within, keeping the catch cool. He even made his own landing nets, shaping the wooden frames, turning the cork handles, and patiently tying every single knot of the mesh. He crafted beautiful wooden fly boxes with tongue-and-groove fittings and filled them with fly patterns of his own design, based on his pioneering study of Northwest trout-stream insects.

Letcher was an old man when I met him, frail and blind, but age had done nothing to dampen the powerful curiosity that had made him such a legendary innovator. We became friends and he invited me to visit the basement workshop at his Seattle home, where he had made all the things for which he was locally famous.

Those visits became frequent and soon evolved into a kind of ritual. The first stop always was the kitchen, where Letcher would mix himself a strong old-fashioned, measuring the portions by feel since he could no longer see the level of liquid in his glass. Then, with one trembling hand clutching the old-fashioned glass and the other unsteadily gripping the handrail, he would start down the steep staircase to the basement workshop while I trailed behind, holding my breath and ready to reach out and catch him if he should miss a step and start to fall. But he knew the route well, having taken it so many times over the years when he could see his way and so many times afterward when he could not, just as he knew the location and contents of every shelf, every cabinet, and every drawer that lined the walls of his workshop.

He would prepare for my visits in the same manner a professor prepares for a class, and when we reached the foot of the stairs there would always be some object or collection of objects arranged on one of the worktables, ready for us to examine. On occasion it might be some of Letcher's fly patterns or those of his friend Preston Jennings, the pioneer eastern fly-fishing entomologist with whom he frequently corresponded and exchanged patterns. He would bring out copies of letters the two had written one another and show them to me, then peer intently through a huge magnifying glass—with such help he could still see the bare outlines of an object—and try to identify each fly pattern, and we would talk about its purpose and design.

Or perhaps we would examine a book or two, removed for the occasion from Letcher's small but distinguished angling library. His wife, Olive, patiently read aloud each new fishing book Letcher acquired after he could no longer see to read them for himself, and little of their contents escaped his memory. He would ask me to look up a passage he recalled and read it, then ask me what I thought of it and whether I agreed with the theory expressed or the observation related, and together we would discuss the proposition and examine it from every angle until we were satisfied we had done it full justice.

But mostly we looked at and talked about bamboo and about Letcher's extraordinary bamboo fly rods. He would ask me to reach up and remove a length of cane from the collection of long, cream-colored shafts stored in the basement rafters, then comment on its color, the sound it made when struck with the haft of a knife, its roundness or lack thereof, the distance between nodes, or the thickness and quality of its pith. From the raw cane he led me through each step of the rod-making process, a complex procedure that required many visits to explain. Early on I recognized that I lacked the talent and skill to do what he had done, but I was still eager to understand it and have the knowledge for its own sake. I also realized I was witnessing a part of angling history and resolved to remember as much of it as I could.

I learned much from those visits, but it was not until later, after Letcher's death, that I discovered just how far he had gone in his search for information about the nature and qualities of rod-making bamboo, or how much he added to our collective knowledge of the subject. His widow, Olive, had given me some of his notebooks, and in one of them—labeled simply BAMBOO—was a collection of faded letters that told a remarkable story.

It began in the 1930s, when Letcher was doing most of his work as a rod builder. Even then there was virtually unanimous agreement that high-quality Tonkin cane was the best material for making rods, but such cane was difficult to obtain. Large commercial manufacturers were the only importers, and they often rejected portions of each shipment as being of inferior quality; amateur builders like Letcher, who had to buy their cane from the commercial manufacturers, frequently ended up with the rejects. This was frustrating, for like every experienced rod builder Letcher knew that even the best craftsmanship could never compensate for inferior materials.

It was this situation that prompted Letcher to begin searching for an independent source of supply. He also wanted to learn more about Tonkin cane—where it came from, how it was grown, the methods used in its harvesting, curing, and processing—so he could include the information in a book he one day hoped to publish. Local libraries provided little information on the subject, so he began writing letters, addressing inquiries to anybody he thought might be able to help. Most of the letters are couched in the formal business language of the day, but they still reveal an extraordinary, sometimes dramatic, and finally poignant tale.

One of the first, dated November 24, 1939, was to Letcher's friend Joe Black, whose family was planning a trip to Indochina (now Vietnam). From its name, Letcher had assumed Tonkin cane was grown in Indochina's Tonkin Province, which prompted the letter.

"Do you suppose that your family would undertake a little mission for me while they are in Indochina?" he wrote. "I want to know about the growth, harvesting, curing, grading and marketing of Tonkin (Tong King) bamboo. . . . I have been trying to get this information for almost two years. It has not been published, and I have not discovered anyone who has first-hand knowledge."

Nearly six months passed before he received an answer. It came in the form of a handwritten letter, unsigned but apparently from a member of Black's family, who said he had been unable to find anyone in Indochina with the information Letcher wanted.

But Letcher hadn't waited. In the meantime he had written to the American consul in Saigon, who referred him to an export firm in Hanoi. A letter to the Hanoi firm elicited a reply written in French, but the notebook contains a handwritten translation:

"We do not handle bamboo for fishing rods at all," the export company wrote, "for the very good reason that Tonkin Province does not export hard bamboo, as this quality could not grow in our climate. Our bamboos are too porous and grow too quickly. They are too large and the interior cavity too considerable to permit any other use of them than in the making of baskets and weaving." The company thoughtfully enclosed "two catalogues of our principal baskets."

The old notebook contains copies of other letters written in late 1939 and early 1940 to other individuals in Indochina, to the American consul general and the British governor of Hong Kong, and to various importers in the United States. In all these Letcher indicated he was still under the impression that Tonkin cane was grown in Tonkin Province in northern Indochina. Then, early in 1940, he received several letters that finally set him straight.

The most detailed was from H. T. Buxton of the Hong Kong General Chamber of Commerce, who told Letcher:

Tonkin canes are grown in the Southern [Chinese] Provinces of Kwangtung and Kwangsi, and the best quality is produced from the Wai Chap [Wai Tsap] district in the latter province. Incidentally, this province borders on French Indochina, which doubtless accounts for their having been named Tonkin canes.

When cut and gathered, the canes are sent to Fatshan, a town some ten miles to the north of Canton, and on the Canton West River. Here is situated the big godowns [warehouses] where the canes are sorted, fired, cleaned and packed, etc., for export.

When ready the canes are shipped by junk to Canton, transferred to river steamers and so brought to Hongkong for transhipment to ocean steamers. . . . This was the shipping procedure up to the Japanese invasion of South China and their capture of Canton, Fatshan, etc. Suffice it to say that on the fall of Canton to the Japanese, all means of communication from outside was cut off for some time and that even today river, road and rail traffic has not been resumed, and consequently direct trade is completely dead.

However, after about a year of trials and tribulation we were able to secure deliveries from stocks in Fatshan against outstanding orders at the time of the Japanese occupation, and these canes were got out by a circuitous route which necessitated coolies carrying the bales for miles across country until finally they reached a portion of the coast not occupied by the Japanese and so were shipped by junk to here. I need hardly enumerate the risks involved of the cargo being captured en route and becoming a total loss, and in addition the coolies on one occasion were machine-gunned from the air by Japanese planes with casualties, and the cargo is at the mercy of every band of Chinese soldiers met with who levy a tax or squeeze on same before letting it proceed. . . . Recently we have again been able to offer these canes to buyers for shipment three to five months after placing of orders, subject to safe arrival of the cargo in Hongkong. Prices, however, show an increase of over 100% over those ruling before the Japanese occupation of South China.

Another letter came from the Hong Kong import-export firm of John Manners & Company. It contained much the same information as Buxton's letter, but added this:

Before the Japanese occupation and blockade of South China, Tonkin canes were exported the whole year round, but in normal times it is recommended to buy as from August onwards for shipment during December until April, as canes harvested in the autumn by the Chinese will be less exposed to rain and consequently better dried by the sun than those cut by the natives during the remaining seasons of the year. The trade will undoubtedly flourish from Canton and Fatshan again the moment the Pearl River has been opened to normal traffic.

The grading for export is in two qualities, First and Second quality. The main characteristics for First quality are:

1. They should be ripe and yellow.
2. They should break with a crack and long splits.
3. No worms and decay.

Second quality, which is inferior to First quality in color (greenish), strength and general appearance, is never exported to U.S.A. . . .

Packing is in grass-mats [tea mats], either single or double packing according to buyer's instructions, and the weight is approx. 250 lbs. per bale for export to America. The number of pieces per bale naturally varies according to the length and the diameter of the canes arranged into a standard packing more or less based on the weight given above.

America is the buyer of the best and most expensive canes from South China, but the final selection of canes suitable for fishing rods is not done here in China but by the manufacturers themselves in England and America, and it appears that these . . . guard with secrecy their source of supply.

Letcher also received a letter from L. B. Wood of Deacon & Company, Ltd., in Canton, whom the American consulate had contacted on his behalf. "We have been established here for one hundred years and are a British firm specializing in the export of South China produce," Wood's letter said. "One of the chief articles of export from South China is bamboo cane, known to the fishing-rod and ski-stick manufacturers as Tonkin cane. . . . We are fully conversant with all details of this business, having regularly exported Tonkin canes to the U.S.A. over a number of years."

The letter repeated the dangers and difficulties of smuggling cane out of Japanese-occupied territory, then added that as a result of these difficulties, "supplies have been something less than one third of normal, but of that third our firm has, without doubt, secured by far the largest part." It also added more details about the growth and harvest of the cane:

Neither growth nor harvesting are regulated, the latter continuing all the year round. . . . After cutting, the canes are washed and dried, but not soaked. As a result of this washing and drying (more particularly the latter) the color changes from green to the pure creamy yellow which exemplifies the genuine Wai Tsap Bamboo. The canes are

then sent to the dealers' godowns, where they are straightened (over charcoal chatties), cut to specified lengths and
baled, prior to export.

Then Letcher received the most important letter of all, from
the American consul in Canton. It enclosed "two bulletins concerning Tonkin cane and other bamboos, prepared by Dr. F. A. McClure
of Lingnan University, Canton. Dr. McClure is considered one of
the outstanding authorities on bamboo. . . ." Here at last was everything Letcher wanted to know about Tonkin cane, contained in two
thin volumes of the 1931 *Lingnan Science Journal,* titled *Studies of Chinese
Bamboos, A New Species of Arundinaria from South China.* One can only
imagine the excitement Letcher must have felt when he opened the
first bulletin and read these words:

> The bamboo which is the subject of the present paper
> is the principal, and practically the only, bamboo exported
> from Southern China. Known as the Tonkin cane of
> commerce, its botanical identity has long remained a
> mystery, and to people in the West even its source was until
> recently unknown.
>
> In 1925 the writer, then in the employ of the U.S.
> Department of Agriculture, learned of its occurrence in
> Kwong Ning and Wai Tsap Districts on the border
> between Kwangtung and Kwangsai Provinces and visited
> this area in an effort to obtain living specimens. With
> some difficulty a few plants were secured. . . . At length, in
> 1929, about 200 plants were secured for transfer to the
> Lingnan University Campus where they have since been
> growing under observation.
>
> This bamboo is known in the West as Tonkin cane,
> among the dealers in China as Ts'ing Lei bamboo and to

the growers and the people generally as Cha Kon Chuk. This multiplicity of names doubtless explains in a measure the confusion that has existed in the West in regard to the origin and identity of this bamboo.

Now that its botanical characters are fully known, it appears that this bamboo falls in the genus *Arundinaria,* of which it represents a species not hitherto described. . . . Since this bamboo is thus far known only in cultivation the question arises as to the wisdom of treating it as a species. Nevertheless, it is so different from any bamboo hitherto described that it should be given a distinctive name. In view of the likelihood that the wild form may be discovered in the course of time, the writer proposes to reserve the specific name *Arundinaria amabilis* (literally "beautiful bamboo") for it. . . .

The remainder of the first volume contained notes and drawings of the botanical characteristics of the cane, along with maps showing the districts where it was grown. The second volume dealt more with its cultivation, handling, and uses. Among the latter, McClure noted, "Western peoples find this bamboo ideally adapted to the manufacture of the highest quality split-bamboo fishing rods."

But he also reported that the quantities of cane grown for commercial harvest were relatively small, and that the growing area was "probably not more than 25 English miles in length, and centering in the little village of Au Tsai."

Within that area, bamboo plantations were established by clearing wild vegetation, McClure wrote, and plants were set out during the first month of the Chinese lunar calendar (usually February). New groves were planted on hillsides, with plants spaced six to ten feet apart. The plants came from an established grove somewhere else; the "propagating material" consisted of "clumps of one or two upright culms with a foot-long portion of the rhizome [rootlike stem] attached."

Once the plant was set in place, the soil was carefully tamped down to cover the rhizome and all other underground parts. This was done to assure "intimate contact" with the soil and the moisture supply—natural rainfall.

"There is usually little sign of growth the first year," McClure wrote. "The appearances are deceitful, however, for the underground part of the plant is steadily growing and extending itself. And in the spring at the end of the first year a few new shoots are sometimes produced."

In good soil a new grove could produce harvestable cane in as little as four or five years, although about ten years were required for a grove to reach maturity. At maturity, McClure observed, the "culms stand stiffly upright even to the tip and are clothed in short, ascending branches and heavy, dark-green foliage." Rhapsodizing over the bamboo as only a botanist could, he remarked on its "austerity and magnificence . . . in striking contrast with the feathery, nodding, ethereal habit of the other, more common bamboos."

McClure reported the largest culm he had seen measured 13 meters (42.6 feet) in height. The cane was harvested year-round whenever individual culms were thought ready. Harvesting was done by workers using heavy, sharp knives, who cut the bamboo, stripped away the leaves and branches, then bundled the culms together and carried them to a nearby stream. There the culms were sorted by size and again tied in bundles. These in turn were made into rafts and floated downstream to a "scouring beach," where women and children scoured each culm with wet sand.

After scouring, the culms were tied in hourglass-shaped bundles and left in the sun, usually for about a week, to bleach and dry,

McClure wrote. Then they were sorted again by size, cut to desired length, and bundled together yet one more time for transportation by boat down the Sui River to Fatshan.

"There are, in Fatshan, six native firms engaged solely in the business of preparing the stems of this bamboo for export," McClure wrote. Most of these had their own large warehouse or storeroom with an adjoining "sunning yard" and a separate building containing firepots, where the culms were straightened to remove crooks or sets. McClure described the process:

> Each worker has a thick-walled earthenware firepot, without a chimney, in which a kind of smokeless coal is burned, a very hot bluish flame playing above the incandescent coals. Two large bricks are laid across the top of the firepot with a space of about 1-$\frac{1}{2}$ inches between them, through which most of the flames pass. The bamboos to be straightened are stacked . . . on the racks which are about a foot above the firepots. Thus they are gradually warmed up. The worker sits on a low stool before his firepot from which position he can reach and pull down the bamboos from the rack without rising. The culms are thrust, one at a time, into the glowing channel between the two bricks, kept there in motion for the brief space of two or three seconds, then withdrawn and subjected to a vigorous straightening process by means of a wooden tool.

Letcher had heard of McClure but had not previously been able to find copies of his published work. He had even tried writing the professor at Lingnan University, but received no reply. The bulletins sent by the American consul in Canton arrived just in time for Letcher to include some of the information in the book he was writing, and when he had finished a draft of his chapter on rod bamboo he decided to try writing McClure again. Somehow he obtained an American mailing address for Lingnan University and wrote to ask if McClure was still associated with the institution.

He received a reply from Olin D. Wannamaker, the university's American director. "Professor F. A. McClure is one of the most important members of our faculty," Wannamaker wrote. "He is continuing his research work in the field of botany, centering at the present time on the study of the bamboo. He is residing on the campus of our university, near Canton. Mail addressed to the campus is subject to delay because of the Japanese censorship. We send our mail in care of the U.S. consul, Canton. . . ."

With that information, Letcher sent a draft copy of his chapter on rod bamboo to McClure in care of the American consul at Canton. "Necessarily, I have drawn freely on your reports, using on many occasions your own language, and I cannot use this chapter unless you are willing to first approve of my doing so," he told McClure in a covering letter. "My manuscript, almost complete except for this chapter, is in the hands of my friend Eugene Connett, proprietor of the Derrydale Press of New York, publishers of fine books on sport. It was written at Connett's request, but has not yet been accepted. . . . Any suggestions or criticism from you on the article will be gratefully received. . . . Whether your decision is favorable or otherwise, please accept my sincere appreciation for the interest you have added to my favorite recreation."

McClure replied three months later.

Your letter . . . reached here last evening, having been forwarded with a large bundle of mail which had been accumulated at Canton. We have been cut off from returning to Canton since the first of September by the action of the Japanese in closing the West River to passenger traffic, and this is the reason for the unfortunate delay in my response to your letter.

I am grateful for the opportunity of seeing your manuscript, and I can appreciate your struggle to get facts. . . .

To me, the techniques followed by the Chinese in producing and handling their economic plant materials are endlessly fascinating, and much more important in many ways than the mere name of the plant, though of course every kind must have its "handle" for practical purposes. I realize that you may be limited as to space and time, but I find myself wishing that you could pass on to your readers something of the spell of the fascination of the operations that go on in the processing mills where the culms are heated and straightened. If I were to have the privilege of talking with you personally, I think I should try to induce you to add some account of this process and the suggestions about what happens to the tissues of the stem when a bamboo is straightened. This could scarcely fail to stir the imagination of the person who is interested in the "Lore of the Split Bamboo." . . .

I have taken the liberty of making a few corrections in your manuscript on the accompanying sheet. I shall look forward to seeing your book when it is out.

Letcher wrote back:

I appreciate your kind letter of November 13 more than I can well express. I will use your suggestion as to the action in the tissues when the culm is heated. . . . I omitted any detailed reference to the straightening of the bamboo by the Chinese intentionally, for the reason that I am inclined to believe that unstraightened culms would be superior. In straightening the whole culm, as the Chinese do, the heat is applied to the enamel surface, with some consequent discoloration and occasional blistering; in straightening the splines in the home workshop, heat is applied to the pith [interior] surfaces, with some charring but without damage to the surface. Also, I have had many culms which had been subjected to too severe heating, so that they were somewhat brittle and fragile, and so useless. I will, of course, be guided by your judgment. . . .

There will be ample time for receipt of your reply. . . . At my request Eugene Connett has released his claim on the manuscript. I made this request because I felt that the information would be of little use to the sportsman who can afford to buy a high-priced book, but that, on the contrary, it would be of considerable service to the much larger body of angler-craftsmen of limited means who must build a fine rod if they want one. . . .

If, as, and when the manuscript is published, it will give me the greatest pleasure to send you a copy.

There is nothing in Letcher's files to indicate whether McClure ever received this letter, or whether he responded if he did. Nor was Letcher ever able to send him a copy of his book, for as events turned out it would not be published in his lifetime.

Ironically, Letcher had learned the origins of Tonkin cane at just about the time all shipments were cut off. The widening war soon put an end to all exports, and rod builders, Letcher included, were forced to rely on supplies already stockpiled in this country.

It was probably for this reason that Letcher started looking for other sources of supply. On February 10, 1940, he wrote to the chamber of commerce in Winter Haven, Florida, saying "a friend told me that considerable bamboo is grown in the vicinity of Winter Haven" and asking if it might include Tonkin cane. The chamber of commerce passed his letter to the county extension agent, who in turn referred Letcher to R. A. Young of the Department of Agriculture's Bureau of Plant Industry in Washington, D.C. Young, the extension agent said, had "made an extensive study of bamboo in this state."

Letcher wrote Young on April 11, 1940:

As a layman, interested in obtaining a better and more uniform quality of bamboo for the making of fine split-bamboo fishing rods, I have conducted an inquiry during the past 2-$^1/_2$ years concerning the growth, harvesting and marketing of the cane exported from Southern China. Both commercial and scientific sources have been most helpful, and I think I now have fairly complete information which I propose to publish as a part of a book dealing with the design and construction of fishing rods and accessories by amateurs. . . .

I would feel that this inquiry has been much more interesting and worthwhile if, as a result thereof, it could be shown that the desired varieties of bamboo are available in commercial quantities in this country, and that methods of harvesting and treating have been developed so as to produce culms comparable with the imported stocks. . . . Any assistance or information you may be willing to supply will be greatly appreciated.

Young responded April 17:

Living plants of the Tsinglee bamboo, *Arundinaria amabilis,* were not brought into the country successfully until some six or seven years ago and the initial propagation has been very slow. The plants which the Department [of Agriculture] was growing took to flowering between one and two years ago and this brought their development practically to a standstill. On the other hand, plants with Mr. E. A. McIlhenny, Avery Island, Louisiana, have not flowered and have multiplied during the last year or two satisfactorily. However, Mr. McIlhenny has recently reported that he does not have stock enough of young plants to offer them to growers as yet. It will be at least six or seven years, we believe, before there will be a supply of culms of sufficient size for use in the making of split fishing rods, even in experimental quantities. . . .

Some makers of split bamboo rods have experimented with other kinds of bamboo and about a year ago we were informed by Mr. E. C. Powell of Marysville, Calif., that after some partially successful attempts he had finally been able to make a high-grade split rod from small culms of the giant timber bamboo, or as it is also known, Japanese timber bamboo, *Phyllostachys bambusoides*. This is a rather hardy species, enduring temperatures down to about 5 degrees F. without appreciable injury. There is a small grove of this at our Plant Introduction Garden, Chico, California, that has produced culms up to about 60 feet high, and another grove on the William S. Tevis Estate, Bakersfield, Calif. There are also a number of young groves of small size scattered over the state, as well as a few, we believe, in Oregon and Washington. There are some old established groves also in the southern states, notably at Avery Island, La., in south central

Alabama, and at our Plant Introduction Garden near Savannah, Georgia.

I believe you would want to assure yourself of the possibility and practicability of making split fishing rods from *Phyllostachys bambusoides* before making any statements in print on the subject. If desired, we could send to you from our Chico Garden (by express collect) an experimental quantity of small or medium-sized culms of this species.

Letcher surely was familiar with the work of E. C. (Edward) Powell, a well-known and innovative craftsman who had been building bamboo rods since about 1910. If Powell had succeeded in making a rod from Japanese timber bamboo, there must be something to it, so Letcher replied immediately to Young and asked him to ship 13 culms, the number he usually ordered from commercial rod-building companies.

Young responded that he had asked the Agriculture Department's Chico garden to "send you as many mature culms of *Phyllostachys bambusoides* as practicable up to 15. . . . We shall be interested in hearing from you as to whether the bamboo culms . . . appear to be as satisfactory as could be expected for that type of bamboo."

On August 9, 1940, Letcher acknowledged receipt of the shipment and expressed his appreciation:

These were received some time ago, just before my departure on a somewhat extended trip, and hence I have not had opportunity to study the material carefully. I think I can best reciprocate your kindness by perfectly frank reports from time to time as the canes are studied and used.

To a rodmaker the first look at these canes is quite disappointing, because they are green and soft, heavily tapered and knobby. The first problem will be to see whether we can cure them. Owing to my absence, I have not been able to sun them, which is probably the correct summer treatment, with regularity. However, they are improving, that is to say, they are turning yellow. I will keep this up for the present, and then try dry storage in the basement.

I do not plan to put them through other tests until they are seasoned and hard. Their roughness will not bother me as some of my best rods have been made of "cranky" culms. However, the groove on the branch side will bother us because we ordinarily make one rod section from a single culm, the six splines having the same relationship as in the original culm. We believe that this preserves a correct balance between tension and compression wood. In the use of this bamboo we will probably find it necessary to assemble the rods with assorted splines.

Two weeks later Letcher sent Young the draft of his book chapter on rod bamboo, the same one he had sent McClure, and asked for Young's comments. He added: "You will be pleased to know that the canes of *P. Bambusoides* are now curing quite rapidly. . . . Also, my friend Harold Stimson has a grove of large bamboos on the grounds of his home at Palo Alto. He has been trying to cut and cure culms for me during the past two years but hasn't worked it out satisfactorily yet." It was Stimson who made the steel planing forms Letcher used in building his rods, and in gratitude Letcher always signed Stimson's name along with his own on each rod he finished.

On August 31, 1940, Young sent Letcher two pages of suggested changes to his chapter on bamboo, most having to do with spelling and taxonomic nomenclature. Letcher thanked him in a September 10 letter, adding:

The specimens of giant timber bamboo that you sent me are curing nicely. It seems that the bleaching occurs to a large extent only in direct sunlight. My friend Stimson has just written me from Palo Alto that he wrapped some string around some culms in his yard when I began to work on bamboo three years ago, and he is now ready to harvest for me. I haven't seen the grove but he tells me they are large culms. . . . He will find it convenient to send the culms to his farm at Tracy, in the Fresno district for curing.

There was no mention of the species of bamboo Stimson was trying to grow and after this there is no further reference to it in Letcher's correspondence, so the outcome of this experiment is unknown.

Further correspondence between Letcher and Young led to the shipment of some older culms from the Chico garden, which Letcher received in October 1941. Letcher allowed these culms to cure for more than two years, then, on January 18, 1944, sent Young a description of their measurements, weight and color.

It will be noted that shrinkage of weight has averaged about 5 percent, and has ranged from nothing to 10 percent. Also, the green tints have entirely disappeared and the color range is from straw to dark straw.

This is, from all appearances, going to be first-class rod bamboo and I am looking forward with great interest to its use. Owing to some rather serious eye trouble, now clearing up, it will probably be one more season before I build the first rod with this material. . . . In due course I expect to make further reports to you.

But Letcher's eye trouble did not clear up. He had diabetes and his eyesight had been damaged beyond recovery. The change can be seen in his notes in the old notebook. His handwriting, once strong and clear, slowly gives way to large, laborious, and increasingly awkward block printing, more and more difficult to decipher, until Letcher finally reached the point where he could no longer either read or write, even with the most powerful magnifying lenses. His days of working with bamboo were over; his long search for a reliable source of Tonkin cane or a good American-grown substitute had ended in the darkness of his own lost sight.

The frustration and bitterness Letcher must have felt over this might have destroyed a man of lesser character, but in the years I knew him he rarely gave any outward sign of distress over his affliction. Nor was he one to give up easily; when he realized he could no longer build rods, he began looking for someone else to whom he might teach his skills.

His first choice was his friend Roderick Haig-Brown, whose reputation as one of North America's great angling writers was just then beginning to take shape, but Haig-Brown demurred, recommending another mutual friend instead. This was Tommy Brayshaw, the well-known British Columbia angling artist and wood-carver.

To Brayshaw, then, went the distinction of building a rod from the cane Letcher had received from the experimental garden in Chico, California. In outward appearance the rod was a work of art, its long straight shafts gleaming with a rich creamy color, but when Letcher handled it for the first time he quickly pronounced it a failure; it lacked the balance, strength, and smooth action he had come to expect and demand from his own rods. The last letter in the old notebook, from Letcher to Brayshaw, blames the failure not on Brayshaw's workmanship but on the quality of the cane. And with this vicarious experiment, Letcher's work came to an end.

In 1973, as editor of *The Flyfisher* magazine, I published Letcher's chapter on rod bamboo—its first appearance in print. Since it revealed much about the cultivation and harvesting of Tonkin cane that never had been reported previously, it has since been quoted widely in many articles and books. That and one other chapter of Letcher's manuscript were the only portions of his book published during his lifetime. He died in 1974.

Five years after his death I prepared and edited the full manuscript of his book, *The Angler's Workshop.* Ironically, it was published in an expensive limited edition—the very reason that Letcher originally withdrew the manuscript from the Derrydale Press—and the publisher failed to make good on a promise to publish a trade edition. Nevertheless, Letcher's chapter on Tonkin rod bamboo remains the most complete account of its growing, harvesting, and processing yet to appear in print.

Letcher Lambuth was a man who felt the passion of split bamboo as few others ever have and it is difficult to imagine all he might have accomplished had blindness not cut short his rod building career. As it was, he made less than three dozen rods, but those few have achieved a degree of fame far out of proportion to their number—a tribute to Letcher's careful craftsmanship and his unique spiral design. It is fitting that he is now remembered for this work, but he deserves equal credit for his long, persistent efforts to uncover and preserve the story of Tonkin cane. To him we owe much of what we now know about the art of raising cane.

CHAPTER ELEVEN

The Write Stuff

Words are the soul and substance of fly fishing. At their best they capture the spirit and excitement of the sport, preserve its collective wisdom, and document its many complex methods and techniques. Words teach, inspire, amuse, entertain, and tell a thousand fishing tales. In magazines and books, pamphlets and circulars, club bulletins and newsletters, and now even on the Internet, words define the essence of the sport. Fly fishing has probably inspired more words in print than any other sporting activity.

That isn't surprising when you consider all the different disciplines involved in fly fishing. Biology heads the list—the biology of fish and the insects and other prey fish feed on—and scores of books are dedicated to these subjects. Then there are the physical disciplines of the sport, casting and wading and all the refinements of each, and these also have inspired many volumes. Fly-tying methods, materials, and patterns are documented in countless books, and the tackle used in fly fishing has accounted for dozens more. Finally, there are books dealing with specific rivers, lakes, or saltwater areas, conservation issues, the history of the sport, or its esthetic and spiritual values, and the number of such titles runs into the thousands.

And they keep coming, more words all the time, an almost daily barrage of new expression on the sport. If one only had the time and patience to read everything in print one could learn something about fly fishing nearly anywhere in the world, keep abreast of all the latest advances in technology and methods, learn and laugh and pass the time doing what many say is the most pleasant thing next to fishing itself—reading about it.

Or maybe not. For the fact that an article or book is about fly fishing does not, in itself, automatically make it worth reading. Anyone who spends very much time perusing fly fishing in print is also bound to find much that is bland, ordinary, pedestrian, and sometimes even barely literate. The truth is that while some writing about fly fishing is as good as writing ever gets, much of it is bad and some of it is downright ugly. That, at least, is my personal appraisal, based on a lifetime of close association with words, including experience as a reader, editor, reviewer, and writer of fly-fishing articles and books.

Much of what now appears in print on the subject of fly fishing is published in magazines. As editor of two such magazines, spaced two decades apart, it has been my opportunity—and occasionally my anguish—to deal with the unedited work of most of the so-called "great" fly-fishing writers of the late 20th century. These are household names in the fly-fishing community, people whose work I had read, respected, and often admired for many years before I became an editor. So perhaps you can imagine my disillusionment when I saw their raw copy for the first time and discovered that many of these "great" writers were so deficient in the basic mechanics of the English language they would have had trouble drafting a short grocery list. Legions of anonymous editors had cleaned up their published work, sometimes even completely rewriting it. There were exceptions, of course, but the reality was that many of these "writers" did not know how to write at all.

This does not necessarily mean they had nothing worthwhile to say; often they did. The problem was they did not know how to say it. That may not be too surprising when you think about it, because while the typical fly-fishing writer spends many years learning to become an expert in some aspect of the sport, he or she rarely spends any time at all learning how to write about it. In this respect fly-fishing writers are little different from the general public; many people assume they were born with a natural talent for expression and all they have to do is sit down at a typewriter or a word processor and immortal prose will automatically follow. Unfortunately it doesn't work that way; even the relatively few people who do have a natural talent for expressing themselves must have training and experience to write well.

I remember the first day of a college writing class when the professor startled all of us students by saying nobody could consider himself a writer until he had written at least 800,000 words. At the time I thought the professor was crazy; now I wonder why he set the figure so low.

The reality is that writing is like casting, or tying flies, or anything else: To become good at it requires constant practice, repetition, study, and refinement. Most people are unable or unwilling to make that sort of commitment, or don't even realize that the commitment needs to be made. And that, probably more than anything else, explains why most magazine writing about fly fishing is of ordinary quality at best; there are limits to what even the finest editors can do to clean it up and make it better.

Experience as an editor also has made me aware of many recurring thoughts and themes in the work of fly-fishing writers. Some of this is to be expected, for while the great diversity of fly fishing provides writers with a wide variety of subjects, the sport has been written about so often by so many for so long that many of its themes have been thoroughly recycled. A large part of an editor's job is to look for a new approach to these old familiar themes.

But that's not all. Editors also must keep an eye out for writers who don't stop at the point of recycling. Plagiarism—the theft of another writer's words—unfortunately is not uncommon among fly-fishing writers. I learned this the hard way, twice as an editor when I unwittingly published material one writer had "borrowed" from another without credit or permission, and several times as an author when my own published work was similarly appropriated by someone else. And I know of several similar episodes involving both fly-fishing magazines and books.

Possibly the writers who commit these offenses think they are merely following in the tradition of Izaak Walton, who borrowed liberally from William Samuel's *The Arte of Angling* to write *The Compleat Angler.* Or maybe they just don't know any better. But literary practices in Walton's time were quite different from those of today, and it's hard to believe any modern writer could not be aware that plagiarism is considered on a par with larceny. Walton also clearly improved on the material he borrowed, while some contemporary fly-fishing plagiarists seem to have difficulty just making accurate copies of the work they purloin.

Plagiarism exists because those guilty of it risk little except possible damage to their reputations, which usually aren't worth much to begin with. This is true because the sums paid for articles in fly-fishing magazines are never large enough to warrant the expense of bringing a plagiarist to justice, which would mean hiring lawyers and going to court. Victims have little recourse other than to try to adopt a charitable attitude toward the offender; in my case, this has meant taking the view that if imitation truly is the sincerest form of flattery, then plagiarism must be the next step beyond flattery.

Not *all* magazine writing about fly fishing is bad, of course. One of an editor's greatest pleasures is to come across the occasional vivid turn of phrase or clever metaphor that makes him wish he'd thought of it himself. Better yet is to find a well-written, thoughtful piece that genuinely sheds new light on some aspect of the sport. The greatest satisfaction of all is to "discover" a good young writer and publish his first work, then watch his skills develop over time. All these things happen just often enough to keep an editor from becoming totally jaded.

A good editor doesn't even really mind all those writers who can't write, either. As long as they're around, it means steady employment.

Magazines, by their very nature, are ephemeral; they come and go like dreams in the night, and like dreams their contents are usually soon forgotten. Books, on the other hand, are permanent. They squat squarely on their shelves like rows of building blocks, which indeed is what they are—the structural, weight-bearing members of the sport of fly fishing. The best books do more than just inform; they lift the reader's spirits, fire his imagination, and bring light to his mind's eye. Probably more books have been published about fly fishing than any other sport, and more new ones are published all the time. No matter what the season, the book hatch is one that never fails.

Why are there so many? The motives are several: Many people write about fly fishing simply from a desire to make money, although in this they are often disappointed; most fly-fishing books sell poorly and return little profit to their authors. Others see books as a way to achieve fame or immortality, although in this, too, they are often disappointed; only a few writers have enduring things to say, or enduring ways of saying them, and even then a generation often must pass before the worth of their work is acknowledged. But a few people write with no expectation of anything at all in return; their only motivation is a genuine love for the sport and a desire to share it with others. It is probably no coincidence that their work is often the best.

The sheer number of fly-fishing books already in print also encourages people to write even more. Writers, especially those just getting started, see the steadily growing number of fly-fishing titles as evidence of a market in constant demand for new material, meaning a market where even an inexperienced writer has a good chance of selling his work. Often that turns out to be the case, so the steady flow of new fly-fishing books stimulates even more of the same, and the cycle feeds on itself.

Publishers often have different motives than writers. Publishers obviously must make a profit to remain in business, so profitability is always a goal. But it is not always the paramount goal; a few publishers are in business primarily because they love good writing and good books, and for them making a profit is only a means to an end. Such publishers are to be cherished. Others, especially those that have been absorbed by one of the giant conglomerates that now dominate the book-publishing industry, have a more mercenary outlook. They may commission a new fly-fishing book to take advantage of a perceived short-term market trend or shift, then just as quickly abandon both the book and its author in favor of the next trend. Quality or originality are usually the least of their concerns, and while they may add to the growing number of fly-fishing titles, they usually add little of distinction.

Some writers publish their own books. Sometimes they do this merely to avoid sharing the profits, if any, with a commercial publisher; sometimes they do it because they could not find a commercial publisher willing to accept their work. Either way, the finished product often lacks professional polish, especially in editing and design, and is automatically considered suspect by people who read lots of fly-fishing books. But some privately published books have turned out to be minor treasures, so they should never be ignored.

As long as fly-fishing books continue hatching with the fecundity of mayflies, there will be many that are no better than ordinary, but there will always be at least some that are good and a few that are outstanding. The very number and diversity of books about the sport assures this. The trick for a reader is to find out which ones are best, and the easiest way to do that is to rely upon an experienced and honest reviewer—if you can find one.

My career as a reviewer began inadvertently shortly after I became editor of *The Flyfisher* magazine in 1972. The established custom was to farm out new fly-fishing books for review by one of a dozen or more writers who contributed to the magazine. This was a practice I tried to continue, but it soon became evident many of the contributors were not very conscientious about meeting deadlines; as a result, I often lacked enough book reviews to fill the space allotted. So, mainly from necessity, I began writing a few reviews myself, just to make sure there would always be enough material to fill the yawning chasms of those empty pages. As time went on I found myself writing more of them, not only to assure a steady supply of material, but also to save on postage—no small consideration in those days of razor-thin magazine budgets.

This continued until Austin Hogan, the late angling historian who was a key adviser and contributor to the magazine, suggested I should write *all* the reviews and publish them in a regular column. This, he said, would establish a degree of consistency that would never be possible as long as I wrote some and assigned others. I could see the merit in his suggestion, but I was reluctant to accept it; in the first place, I had never really wanted to be a book reviewer, and in the second, writing a regular column was a bit more work than I had bargained for when I signed on as editor. In time, however, the continuing problem of getting other reviewers to submit their work on schedule finally convinced me to give Austin's idea a try, so I wrote and published a couple of experimental columns and sat back to await response. Somewhat to my surprise, the response was positive, so I decided, reluctantly, to keep on writing the column—never guessing it would continue for 18 years.

Early on I discovered that being a book reviewer was some people's idea of a dream job; after all, a reviewer gets all those free books, and what better deal could you possibly want? I also heard from many people who thought reviewers were lowly, vicious parasites, the scum and dregs of society, whose only satisfaction came from savaging the work of starving, helpless writers. Both views are grossly mistaken.

It is true that reviewers do get lots of free books, but the problem is they must also *read* all of them, good or bad, page after interminable page, taking notes all the while, and then try to think of something clever or meaningful to say about them so readers will have a basis for deciding which ones they might like. It doesn't take long to discover that the difference between reading books for pleasure and reading them because you *must* is the dividing line between enjoyment and hard work, and my relationship with books has never been quite the same since I became a reviewer. As for all those "free" copies, I admit there are still a few in my library, but most—better than 90 percent—have been donated to fly-fishing or conservation groups for fund-raising auctions or raffles.

Those who believe reviewers are parasites are often authors themselves or the friends and relatives of authors, especially those who have felt the painful thrust of a reviewer's pen. And believe me, having felt it myself a couple of times, I know nothing else hurts quite as much—unless it's a kidney stone. Yet many fly-fishing writers misunderstand the reviewer's role, partly because few have a literary background to begin with and partly because fly-fishing books have largely escaped meaningful criticism throughout most of the sport's history.

The reviewer's role, at least as I have always conceived it, is twofold: first to serve as a consumer advocate, giving praise for quality and warning for shoddy goods, and second to be part of the cultural winnowing process that helps establish the literary value of new works. The first of these responsibilities is straightforward—it involves nothing more than letting people know whether a book is worth their time and money. It's the second that causes most of the confusion.

Perhaps the best way to explain it is to compare the book reviewer's task with the process of scientific peer review: When a scientist prepares to publish the results of a research project or announce a major discovery, it is customary for his or her work to be submitted to other experts in the field, who try to evaluate the quality of the research or replicate its findings. Their collective judgment largely establishes the worth of the scientist's work. A similar process is followed in music, film, literature, and art: Each new work is scrutinized by critics, who apply the benefit of their experience and knowledge and render an opinion, and it is largely the consensus of these opinions that determines whether a work is considered a masterpiece or consigned to obscurity. This sort of cultural trial by jury may not be perfect, but it is the best method society has yet devised for establishing a fair measure of the value of artistic things. And the critic's part is essential.

But it has rarely worked that way for books about fly fishing. Before the 1970s, angling-book criticism was in a pitiful state. What passed for book reviews in those days was usually little more than mutual back scratching by an old boys' network of writers for large, general-circulation outdoor magazines. They had nothing but good things to say about their colleagues' latest books, and their "reviews" were written with the clear expectation that the author whose work was being praised would soon return the favor. Seldom was heard a discouraging word.

Only the late Arnold Gingrich and one or two others ever dared to say in print what they really thought of some of the new fishing books. Gingrich, as publisher of *Esquire,* was accustomed to the real world of literary criticism, where reviewers normally say exactly what they think—sometimes with all the subtlety of a heavy-weight boxer—but his published criticism of a fishing book came as a shock to many in the angling community; people seemed to think it was somehow impolite or unseemly.

Other reviewers have since tried to follow Gingrich's example, and one result is that your chances of reading an honest, thoughtful, meaningful review of a fly-fishing book are better now than they would have been 25 years ago. But only a little better; candid reviews of fly-fishing books are still the exception rather than the rule, and the mutual back-scratching school of reviewers is far from dead.

As a disciple of Gingrich, who was a colleague and adviser, I have always tried to follow his example. On occasion this has meant questioning the work of people I considered friends; sometimes they took it personally, costing me their friendship. Others reacted indignantly, as if they thought their work should remain above criticism—

that their prose, however labored, or their pronouncements, however pedestrian, ought to be passed on without question to the waiting fly-fishing masses.

One writer I took to task for claiming credit for a "discovery" others had described decades earlier reacted by challenging me to a duel. A couple of others, whose books I had reviewed in less-than-glowing terms, later counterattacked in print when given an opportunity to review books that I had written or edited—the flip side of the old mutual back-scratching approach. Another author, whose work I reviewed favorably, wrote to thank me, but wondered in passing if I knew I had been given a nickname by writers whose books I hadn't liked as much; they called me "The Torch," he said. I wrote back to say it was nice to be called a five-letter name for a change.

I might have been the only reviewer who didn't like Norman Maclean's *A River Runs through It,* which has practically become a fly-fishing icon. My dislike was based on some of the book's fly-fishing scenes, which didn't ring quite true to me, and I was disturbed by its almost gratuitous use of profanity; for those reasons I elected not to review it. Later, when I started reading the high praise of others, I thought I might have missed something, so I went back and took a second look at the book, which only confirmed my original feelings. There may indeed be a wonderful story hidden in those pages, but if so it has remained hidden from me.

I did enjoy the movie, though.

Whenever I decided to pass up a book for review, as in the case of *A River Runs through It,* I rarely got any letters questioning my judgment; those kinds of letters usually came after I *did* write a review. Not all were plaintive, however; the responses of many authors indicated they clearly understood the purpose and value of the review process even if they did not always agree with the results, and most knew better than to take the results personally. I also received many kind and thoughtful letters from readers, which I took as evidence that they had grown to expect and appreciate candid appraisals of new books. I hope they will never settle for less.

After having been a reviewer so many years, I think I can now say what qualifications a reviewer of fly-fishing books ought to have— and they begin with a thick skin. But a good reviewer also must have a broad and thorough knowledge of the sport, the kind of knowledge that can only be gained by many years of actual fly-fishing experience and reading. A good reviewer must respect the language, be comfortable with it in all its subtle nuances, and be willing and able to express himself. He should always be prepared to offer praise when it is due and equally ready to condemn mediocrity, yet he must also be very careful never to accuse an author of having failed at something it was not the author's intention to do. Above all, a reviewer must always try to be fair.

It helps greatly if a reviewer has written books himself and had them reviewed, for nothing else can make him better understand the effort or the passion required to bring a book to life, or how it feels to have one's work criticized in public. That kind of understanding will help him wield a gentler pen.

Finally, a good reviewer must always be honest, truthful, and have the courage to state his opinions, and he should write for a publication with the same set of virtues.

A book reviewer learns not to expect much in the way of rewards, but the job does offer the occasional satisfaction of discovering a new book of rare excellence—one with an unusual quality of thought or expression, or sometimes both. Such books are to be savored; they make reading a pleasure rather than a task, and they leave the mind with a pleasant aftertaste, like fine wine hovering on the tongue. Sometimes the pleasure of discovery is doubled if the author is someone new, his book the first echo of what is clearly destined to be a major voice.

Over time I have encountered a number of such writers who have become favorites. Their names make a short list, but one that I offer in the confident expectation that anyone who reads their books will not be disappointed. They include David James Duncan, John Gierach, W. D. Wetherell, Harry Middleton, Steven J. Meyers, and M. R. Montgomery. I did not "discover" Nick Lyons or William Humphrey—they were already writing books before I started reviewing them—but I have always welcomed every new title from each, and I recommend them with the same confidence. I continue reading fly-fishing books in the hope of finding more writers like these.

The term *literature* is often applied to fly fishing books, but usually in a quantitative sense, meaning all the books published about the sport. Only rarely is it applied in a qualitative sense, meaning works of permanent value, excellence in form, or great emotional impact. That's because only a few fly-fishing books have ever been able to meet the qualitative definition, and these have never been considered serious literature. The generally sorry state of fishing-book criticism is surely one reason why.

That's why we need more reviewers with the experience to make good judgments and the courage to speak plainly. Only when we have them, and only when each new fly-fishing book is appraised with the same honesty and candor now applied to most books outside the realm of sport, can we expect the best fly-fishing books will be admitted to the ranks of serious literature.

But make no mistake about it: That's where they belong.

CHAPTER TWELVE

From Abbey to Zulu

You probably won't find Alaska Mary Ann, Hairy Mary, or Big Bertha on the centerfolds of *Playboy*. But you might find them in a fly box.

The names of these fly patterns, and many others like them, are part of the longest and most colorful roster in all of sport. There are at least 10,000 published patterns and probably as many more known only to their creators and a few friends, countless dressings scribbled on cocktail napkins or the backs of envelopes and stuffed away in moldy fishing vests. They begin with Abbey and end with Zulu, and many of their names are even more colorful or imaginative than the patterns themselves.

Fly tiers have a long tradition of christening flies with unusual or beautiful names. One reason they do so is esthetic—most good fly tiers rightfully consider themselves artists, and artistic creations deserve something more than just an ordinary name. Another reason is economic—when flies are tied for the commercial trade, those with colorful names (as well as colorful dressings) have a better chance of selling. If you don't believe that, then suppose you had to choose between a Pink Lady and a Brown Grub. You get the idea.

Fly-pattern nomenclature has come a long way since the first definitive written record of an artificial fly appeared in Aelian's *De animalium natura* in the third century A.D. Writing of "a Macedonian way of catching fish," Aelian described how the Macedonians fastened red wool around a hook and attached "two feathers which grow under a cock's wattles, and which in color are like wax" to imitate a fly they called Hippouros. It wasn't much of a fly, and certainly not much of a name, but it was a beginning.

After Aelian there was a literary gap of many centuries until the appearance in 1496 of *The Treatyse of Fysshynge wyth an Angle*, attributed to a shadowy figure known as Dame Juliana Berners. The *Treatyse* listed a dozen fly patterns and recommended when to use them on British trout streams. It was obvious this information had taken a long time to develop, indicating that fly fishing and fly tying had been evolving in England for a considerable time even though it had not been mentioned previously in any book that still survives. Even so, the names of flies in the *Treatyse* lacked imagination by modern standards. They included a couple of "Dun Flyes," a "Stone Flye," a "Ruddy Flye," a "Yellow Flye," and a "Tandy Flye." Only one of the 12 had a name that might have earned it a second glance on a modern tackle-shop counter, and that was the "Blacke Louper" (leaper).

Nevertheless, these 12 flies were disciples for the infant sport, providing the foundation for what has become a rich fly-tying tradition that has produced many beautiful patterns bearing equally beautiful names—the Iron Blue Dun, Greenwell's Glory, Lunn's Particular, Pale Morning Dun, Tup's Indispensable, and Welshman's Button, to mention just a few.

After fly fishing spread to the New World, North Americans got into the act with a host of original names of their own. Among the best: Parmachene Belle, Afternoon Delight, Coquihalla Orange, Fall Favorite, Rusty Rat, Dean River Lantern, Warden's Worry.

For as long as I can remember these names have fascinated me. I can still vividly recall the names of the first flies my father gave me as a boy, when we were fishing the Kamloops trout lakes of British Columbia: Colonel Carey, Black O'Lindsay, Nation's Special, Cummings Fancy, Lioness, and others. I remember wondering who

Colonel Carey was, and imagining a spare, lean, straight-backed figure with a pencil-thin military mustache, dressed in a sharply pressed British officer's uniform and carrying a riding crop. I loved the lyrical way the name *Black O'Lindsay* came tumbling off my tongue, and recall puzzling over how a fly ever could have gotten a name like that (much later I learned it was named after Judge Spencer Black of Lindsay, California). I remember wondering whether Nation was a country or a person, who was this Cummings fellow who gave us his Fancy, and why anyone would call a fly the Lioness (we have met Bill Nation elsewhere in these pages, but I never did learn the history of the Cummings Fancy or the Lioness).

While I wondered about their origins, I also sensed the importance of these names and others like them, recognizing them as part of the peculiar nomenclature of fly fishing. Fly-pattern names are among the things that define the sport, setting it apart from all others and giving it an exclusive language all its own. If you hear someone talking about Hendricksons, Gray Ghosts, Red Quills, or Silver Doctors, and you don't have to ask for a translation, then you speak fly fishing.

Although fly fishing always has been something of a rule-bound sport, there are as yet no rules for naming new fly patterns. Some flies are named on the spur of the moment, frequently to honor a person, place, or thing, but others are christened only after long and thoughtful consideration. Some names are chosen purposely in the hope of giving a new pattern a label as artful as its appearance, and some are selected in a conscious effort to gain some sort of angling immortality for the author of the fly. All such names are legitimate and traditional, and because they stem from such different motivations, they contribute to the kaleidoscopic variety of names that fill the pattern books. They are adornments to the sport, like ornaments on a Christmas tree.

The names of some fly patterns make their origins or inspirations inherently obvious—what better example than the famous Skykomish Sunrise?—but the names that intrigue me most are the ones that aren't so obvious, those that raise more questions than they answer. What fascinating set of circumstances could have inspired the naming of the '52 Buick? Why would someone call a fly the House and Lot? What tale could have prompted a tier to christen his fly the Family Secret? Was the Bouncer named for a pattern that bounces over riffles, or after some big guy who throws people out of bars? It's probably safe to assume that Dan Quayle didn't name the Potato Nymph, but if he didn't, then who did? And why did he or she call it that?

Many flies have been named after royalty. Starting with the Royal Coachman, probably the best-known fly in the universe, you can work all the way up the royal pecking order with patterns named after lords, ladies, chamberlains, princes, queens, and kings. This tradition may stem from the days when royalty and nobility controlled the best fishing in the British Isles; what better way to assure friendly relations with the local lord, and perhaps gain permission to fish his private water, than to name a fly pattern after him?

Flies named after military officers—captains, majors, colonels, generals, admirals, and the all-encompassing Brass Hat—are common, but the same is not true for enlisted men; I don't know of a single pattern named after a private, corporal, sergeant, or petty officer. Other patterns are named for doctors (Silver Doctor, Surgeon General, Quack Doctor, General Practitioner), lawyers (Bronson's Barrister, Old Judge), and Indian chiefs (Bannock Chief, and so on). Clergymen also receive their due (Cardinal, Bishop, Priest, Missionary, Deacon, several Saints), as do their adversaries (Witch, Devil, Demon, Presbyterian Killer).

There are flies named after various political offices (Governor, Supervisor, Premier, Improved Governor), academicians (Professor, Proctor), corporate managers (Boss, Supervisor, Tycoon), and many different trades (Butcher, Flagger, Potter, Shoemaker, Undertaker, Vamp, Candlestick Maker, Pink Floozy). Not surprisingly, several fly patterns also bear the names of cocktails (Tequila Sunrise, Bloody Mary, Mai Tai, Whiskey & Soda), which might have helped inspire them.

Many fly patterns are named after cities (Belgrade, Chicago, Laramie, Manchester, Montreal, Portland, Walla Walla, and Oconomowoc, to mention just a few). Many others have states in their names (Arizona, California, Idaho, Montana, Utah, Colorado, New Mexico, Connecticut, Wyoming).

Some patterns bear mysterious names (Black Dose, Gray Ghost, Coffin Fly, Mystery). Other names defy ready explanation (Grumpy, Polka, Studley, Albino Moose), and some are merely revolting (Maggot, Cowdung, Bloody Butcher, Dead Chicken, Rat-Faced MacDougal).

There is even a fly called the Lady Godiva. One might suppose it's only a bare hook, but it's actually a handsome steelhead fly.

There are a few saltwater fly patterns with glamorous names (Platinum Blonde, Blackberry Blossom, Old Glory, Crazy Charlie, Electric Anchovy, Prince of Tide, Surf Candy) but many more with names that seem hopelessly commonplace (Ray's Tarpon Fly, Jack's Shrimp, Cal's Anchovy, and the like). Saltwater fly tiers need to exercise more imagination.

Alliteration always has been a popular device in naming fly patterns and has given us such wonderful appellations as the aforementioned Rusty Rat, Warden's Worry, and Fall Favorite, plus the Bishop's Blessing, Spectral Spider, Fraudulent Friend, Dappled Dog, and many more.

From its origins in the British Isles and North America, the tradition of colorful and imaginative names for flies has spread around the world, wherever flies are tied. The large feathered lures created by New Zealand tiers have intriguing names like Craig's Night-Time, Green Sleeves, Hamill's Killer, Red Setter, and Mrs. Simpson. Tasmanian anglers have their Woolly Pup, Nymbeet, Noel's Nobby, Snow Burner, and Yeti. The French have the Assassine, Bourrue du Rhône, Loge-Coucou, Plantureuse, and Tricolor. And so on.

Yet despite this long tradition of lively names, there are disturbing signs that many modern tiers are beginning to abandon the practice. More and more it seems that when a tier creates a new pattern he or she names it something dull and simple, like Dave's Green Bug or Joe's Special. Other tiers, striving for the elusive goal of exact imitation, christen their patterns after the insects they are intended to imitate, which gives us such bland, generic names as the Green Drake and Olive Damselfly Nymph. Yet other tiers, suffering a similar or even worse lack of imagination, name their flies after the materials or style of tying used in them. Thus we have the Olive Seal's Fur Nymph, Rubber Legs Nymph, Parachute Cahill, No-Hackle Dun, and so on.

Worse yet are tiers who insist on assigning to their patterns the Latin names of insects they are supposed to imitate, such as *Paraleptophlebia* Dun or *Siphlonurus* Nymph.

Fortunately, this unimaginative trend so far seems limited mostly to trout patterns, mainly dry flies and nymphs, and hasn't yet spread to wet-fly or streamer patterns. And since Atlantic salmon and steelhead flies rarely resemble anything in nature, they continue to have names that reflect the wildest flights of imagination—Blue McGoon, Cosseboom, Green Highlander, Night Dancer, Purple Bad Habit, Egg-Sucking Leech, and so on.

Such fanciful names ought to be encouraged; the more of them, the better. Other sporting activities have their own terminologies and some have traditions that go back at least as far as those of fly fishing, but nothing else has anything quite like the argot of the artificial fly. What other sport could offer the Shaving Brush, Sassy Cat, Rich Widow, Mormon Girl, Silver Fairy, Wickham's Fancy, or December Gold? Where else could you conjure up the images such names evoke?

And of course the names are only part of it; each name also denotes a unique recipe of fur, feathers, or other exotic materials, often collected from the far corners of the world; each also has its own history of trial and error, of testing and fine-tuning, and finally of success on some storied lake or stream. And each has its own place, however large or small, in the lore and legend of fly fishing.

Be glad for the names of flies; there is nothing else quite like them anywhere. If you should ever add a pattern of your own to this historic list of dressings, make certain you christen it properly with a name that is colorful, imaginative, or alliterative—or, better yet, all three.

PART IV

Reality and Fantasy

CHAPTER THIRTEEN

Getting Stoned

One of the more common bits of bumper-sticker wisdom you see around these days is the observation that the worst day of fishing is better than the best day of work. As a philosophical statement the truth of that seems unassailable, and for most of my life I embraced it enthusiastically; to me there never was any doubt that the worst day of fishing *was* better than the best day of work.

That was true even for those fishing days when things went wrong—when tires went flat, engines refused to start, rod tips were broken, there was too much wind or rain, mosquitoes were unbearable, or something vitally important was forgotten and left behind. Even on those occasions it was still unquestionably far better to be out fishing, in pursuit of wild creatures amid the glories of water, earth, and sky, than to be cooped up in a stuffy office struggling with the petty politics and largely artificial problems of the day-to-day business world.

But then came an incident that reminded me forcibly of the truth of another old saying: For every rule there is an exception. It was a day I would rather have been almost *anywhere* else than where I was, which was fishing.

Not that things started off badly. The morning air was fresh and full of promise as we drove into Dry Falls Lake, at the bottom of a great stone amphitheater carved by the Ice Age falls of the Columbia River, the mightiest waterfall the earth has ever known. At the foot of the cliffs where the water of the prehistoric Columbia once thundered now lies a deep basin filled with water, rimmed by extensive shallows and a long, thin, shallow arm that stretches southward into the desert. These rich, weed-filled shallows often have been likened to a chalk stream without a current, and they harbor large, sometimes difficult trout. That combination, plus the spectacular scenery, has long made Dry Falls one of my favorite places. I'd experienced many memorable days there—including one when I was caught in the ash fall from the explosion of Mount St. Helens—but nothing had prepared me for what was about to happen on this day.

I had fished the lake a week earlier, trying out a new fly pattern, a chironomid imitation I had been fussing with for some time. The latest version had been a stunning success; the normally wary trout had taken it as if they were chocolate junkies and the fly was an M&M. I had brought only a few of the new patterns and the trout chewed them down almost to bare hooks, so I had rushed home to tie more. Now I was back with the whole family, and the plan for the day was that Randy and I would fish while Joan and our daughter, Stephanie, went horseback riding.

I was anxious to start fishing, confidently expecting to duplicate the success of the new fly pattern, so Randy and I quickly unloaded our cartop boats from the truck, gathered up our gear, and waved good-bye to Joan and Stephanie, who drove off in the truck. Then, with our fly rods rigged up and a couple of the new patterns tied to our leaders, Randy and I rowed swiftly to the spot in the shallows where I'd had such good fishing a week earlier.

When we got there I could see large trout cruising along the edge of a weed bed in clear, shallow water, and started casting to them. A couple came and looked at my new fly but then turned away; the others did not respond at all. I thought their strangely indifferent behavior might be due to the absence of a chironomid hatch; surely when the water warmed up a little more the hatch would begin, and then the fish would start taking as avidly as they had the week before.

But an hour passed and still there was no hatch; the trout remained disinterested and neither Randy nor I had been able to tempt one. Meanwhile, I was beginning to feel a little strange, a sort of dull, heavy feeling deep inside. Then I noticed the beginning of a vague pain in my lower right back. It felt like a muscle strain, and at first I tried to ignore it, but the pain increased and became steady and soon was sharp enough to be bothersome. I tried stretching to relieve it, but that only seemed to make it worse.

By then the sun was full upon the water and still there was no hatch. I decided it was time to try fishing somewhere else, so I told Randy I was going to head for the south arm of the lake. Maybe the trout there would be feeding, and maybe the half-mile row would warm up the muscles in my back and ease the annoying pain.

Randy decided to stay behind, so I started off alone. Very soon it became apparent that rowing wasn't going to ease the pain; on the contrary, it seemed to get worse with every stroke of the oars. By this time I realized it was not a simple muscle strain; this was serious, major-league pain. It felt as if someone had driven a hot soldering iron into my back and was twisting it around, and just when I thought it couldn't possibly get any worse, it got worse. I was starting to sweat and there was a flat, metallic taste in my mouth.

But I wasn't about to quit. I don't get very much time to go fishing—at least I didn't then—and I was determined that no damned pain was going to drive me off the water. Besides, it had come on very quickly and might leave just as quickly as it came. So I took a deep breath, clenched my teeth, and kept rowing.

The pain got worse and I had to stop and rest. It was becoming the worst pain I could remember, beyond anything I had thought it possible to experience. I could close my eyes and see the pain, a white-hot hole burning in the darkness, throbbing and pulsing and glowing with every tortured breath I took. Yet I was determined not to let it beat me. In fits and starts, pausing frequently to rest, I kept rowing, slowly making my way down the narrow channel leading to the south arm.

When I reached the end of the channel, where it opened into a wide bay, I was all alone. I paused again to rest, letting the boat drift before the gentle breeze. The pain closed in again, even worse than before. Tears leaked from my eyes and my breath came short as a spasm of pain seized my whole body and shook it like a dog playing with a bone. I tried desperately to find some posture or position that might offer momentary relief, but there was no escape from the relentless pain.

I forgot about fishing, or about going any farther. Every move brought a fresh assault of pain. I knew whatever was causing it must be serious, and for the first time realized I needed help. But there was no one else around, and by now I was hurting far too badly to think of rowing all the way back.

The only chance seemed to be to go ashore and try to make my way back on foot. Even that wouldn't be easy; the south arm of Dry Falls is surrounded by dense brush and thick tules that grow higher than a man's head, and there are very few places where it's possible to go ashore. I knew of only one, a spot where other anglers had beaten a path through the brush to the water's edge. Gritting my teeth so hard I thought they would fracture, I took up the oars again and with feeble, pain-filled strokes headed for the spot.

It couldn't have been more than a couple of hundred yards, but it seemed to take an hour to get there. When the bow of the boat finally grated on the shore, the thought of getting to my feet was more than I could bear, so I crawled over the bow toward the narrow path that beckoned through the brush.

I had gone no more than a couple of feet on my hands and knees when I came face to face with a wall of poison ivy. There was no doubt about what it was; the sticky, glistening leaves were poised in waiting clusters, ready to add to my misery. I stared at the stuff, trying to will it to go away, but of course it wouldn't. The only thing to do was try to get up on my feet and go around it.

Gritting my teeth yet again, I pushed myself unsteadily to my feet; the pain immediately increased on a logarithmic scale. By now I had a pretty good idea what it was; I'd heard that kidney stones are perhaps the most painful of all human afflictions, and I couldn't think of anything else that might have gone wrong in that portion of my anatomy. If I was right, the good news was that it probably wasn't fatal; considering how I felt at the moment, that was also the bad news.

Getting up had made me dizzy, so I stood still for a moment and waited for the spinning horizon to settle down. When it did, I started forward, picking my way slowly through the poison ivy, trying to place each foot carefully to avoid contact with the stuff.

I'd taken only a few steps when I saw the rattlesnake, coiled and waiting beneath my upraised foot.

In a far-off corner of my mind where the pain had yet to reach I had the quick thought that if I wasn't hurting so badly I'd probably be laughing just then. What more could possibly go wrong?

After that I don't remember much about what happened. The snake and I evidently went our separate ways and I have a dim recollection of seeking shade behind a huge basalt boulder left behind by the prehistoric floods, then writhing on the ground in an unsuccessful attempt to find some position that would relieve the pain. Nobody was around and I realized my idea of seeking help on foot was hopeless; it was nearly a mile across the desert to the nearest road and I knew I would never be able to make it that far. After a while, unable to think of anything else to do, I made my way slowly and painfully back to the boat.

That's where Randy eventually found me, hanging over the side, desperately ill and almost delirious with pain. I had been gone so long he had gotten worried and come looking for me. Sizing up the situation quickly, he tied his anchor rope to the bow of my boat and started rowing frantically back toward the launching area, towing my boat behind him. I stretched out in the bottom of the boat, too sick and overcome with pain to appreciate the fact that he was in the process of breaking the world rowing-speed record. He didn't even bother to beach his boat when we reached the launching point; instead, he jumped into the water and rushed ashore to find help.

He found two other anglers who offered to drive us somewhere we could get assistance. They helped me into the back of their van and we started over the rough, rocky road leading away from Dry Falls. The ride was excruciating, with every jolt triggering a fresh spasm of pain that exploded in my back and radiated outward all the way to my fingertips.

The anglers drove to a ranger station in the nearby state park and one hurried inside to find the ranger while his companion and Randy helped me out of the van. I stretched out on the soft, cool grass of the ranger's well-kept lawn and closed my eyes, only vaguely aware of the circle of people who gathered to stare at me curiously.

The ranger phoned for a medic unit. When it arrived Randy climbed in front while the paramedics loaded me on a gurney, wheeled it into the back of the aid car, and clamped an oxygen mask over my face. Then, to the accompaniment of a siren's mournful rise and fall, we started on the 20-mile run to the nearest hospital.

At the hospital an X ray confirmed my suspicion of what was wrong: The film showed the ghostly image of a kidney stone looming like a full moon on a foggy night. It felt as large as the full moon, too. A doctor, somewhat irritated because he had been summoned off the local golf course, examined the X ray and confirmed the diagnosis. He wrote a prescription for some pain medicine, told me to go home and see my own doctor, and headed back to the golf course.

Going home and seeing my own doctor was more easily said than done. Joan and Stephanie were still 20 miles away with the truck, and as far as Randy and I knew they had no idea where we were. But it turned out the park ranger had gotten in touch with the local sheriff, who had found them and told them what had happened. I was still lying on a gurney in the emergency room, wondering what to do next, when they drove up in the truck. I crawled painfully into the back of the pickup and we stopped at a drugstore to fill the prescription for pain medication before starting on the four-hour trip back over the Cascades to our home in Seattle. The medication had no discernible effect on the pain, and the trip was a journey of agony beyond measure.

It was late when we reached home and I rested while Joan called the doctor, who told her to get me quickly to the hospital. She brought our car around to the front of the house, helped me out the front door, down the sidewalk, and into the car, and we drove to the emergency room. We were met by a squadron of attendants, who put me in a wheelchair and wheeled me to the admissions counter.

I was sitting in the wheelchair, answering questions from the admitting nurse, when Joan leaned over and whispered, "Don't look now, but I think you stepped in something on the way to the car."

I looked anyway, and she was right. The sidewalk in front of our house is a popular dog-walking area, and—well, you get the picture.

I had wanted to know what more could possibly go wrong. Now I had the answer.

I remained in the hospital three days while the doctors pumped me full of liquids, trying to get that stubborn stone to move, but it remained stuck firmly where it was. Surgery was finally necessary to remove it, and that meant another week in the hospital. Then painful complications developed and I nearly had to have surgery a second time. That was avoided at the last minute, but then I got an infection and there were more complications, and in the end it was a full month before my internal plumbing started functioning normally again. By then I was feeling pretty weak and worn down and the doctor wasn't enthusiastic when I suggested a week of fishing might be just the thing to bring me around.

I went anyway, against his advice. Not to Dry Falls—I wasn't quite ready to go back there just yet—but to Oregon, where I fished for a week, took it easy, and felt a lot better afterward. Nothing bad happened, either; whatever cloud had been parked over my head that day at Dry Falls seemed to have moved on.

Now, whenever I see one of those bumper stickers that says the worst day of fishing is better than the best day of work, I smile to myself and think, yes, that's certainly true—but I can think of one exception.

CHAPTER FOURTEEN

Dame Juliana's Slide Show

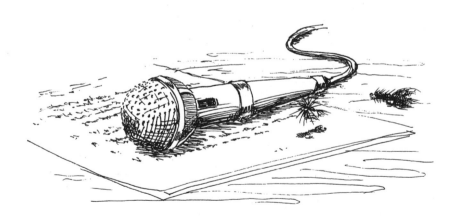

If Dame Juliana Berners were alive today she would have a slide show. She would travel around the country, showing her slides at fly-fishing conclaves, outdoor shows, and club meetings. She would also have a series of casting videos, a "signature" line of fishing clothes, her own mail-order catalog, and her own Web site. Her name would be on the mastheads of several fly-fishing magazines, she would have at least a couple of books to her credit, and she would have her own fly-fishing school. She would be a guest on the Saturday-morning outdoor television shows and would lead tours to posh fishing resorts in exotic locales. That's what a thoroughly modern Juliana would be like.

Or perhaps it's not fair to suggest that the legendary prioress of Sopwell Nunnery, credited with writing the first treatise on fly fishing in the English language, could be so blatantly commercial. After all, it was she who admonished that "you must not use this . . . artful sport for covetousness, merely for the increasing or saving of your money, but mainly for your enjoyment and to procure the health of your body and, more especially, of your soul."

But if not Dame Juliana, then we could just as easily choose another angling pioneer—someone such as Walton ("Would someone in the audience like to come forward and play the role of Venator?"), Cotton, Halford, Gordon, or any number of others—to make the point: The point being that whatever fly fishing once was, it has lately become a big business, with all the trappings of same.

Fly fishing has been commercialized, computerized, containerized, conglomerated, shrink-wrapped, and Madison-Avenueized. It has become a darling sport of the Baby Boomers, a badge of status for up-and-coming yuppies, an outdoor mantra for the slightly weird. Many people have been drawn to the sport by its genuine appeal, but others have joined up for different reasons: a perception of status, for the sake of their "upper-body cardiovascular health," or because they think it's cool to be seen in the latest fly-fishing fashions from L. L. Bean and Orvis.

Whatever the reasons, fly fishing is now a big industry. Back in the 1940s, when I started fishing, anglers worried about their fly lines, which required careful dressing before use; now it seems more of them worry about their bottom lines.

How did this happen? A historian would be hard pressed to point to a certain date and say "This is when it all began." Like many societal changes, its origins can be traced to subtle economic and technological shifts whose beginnings are difficult to detect. But in retrospect we can see clearly that economic prosperity created more leisure time, and this, coupled with the population increase brought about by the Baby Boom, created a rapidly growing market. At the same time, different and more effective means of advertising, communication, and travel were coming on line, and as these and other currents gathered momentum they simultaneously began to converge.

The early 1970s probably can be pinpointed as the time they all came together, and they met with a flash like self-igniting rocket fuel. The result wasn't just an explosion; it was a supernova. Fly fishing began an incredible period of expansion in public and commercial popularity that has yet to reach its bounds.

Some results of this expansion are easy to measure. In 1970 North America had only two magazines dedicated exclusively to fly fishing or fly tying, and neither was more than two years old; today there are at least 11 such magazines. Before 1970, book publishers paid only occasional attention to fly fishing, but the next decade saw a proliferation of fly-fishing titles unprecedented in the history of sport; now at least six publishers dedicate most or all their output to fly-fishing, while others publish at least a few fly-fishing titles to balance their trade lists. In 1970 there were perhaps four or five major mail-order catalog firms specializing in fly-fishing tackle and fly-tying materials; now there are dozens. Commercial fly-fishing schools were rare in 1970; now there is at least one and usually several in every angler's neighborhood.

Before 1970 outdoor trade shows were uncommon; those catering to fly fishers were more uncommon still. Now there is at least one major show in virtually every metropolitan area of the country. Hundreds of fly-fishing clubs have been established since 1970, and things that were then only a twinkle in the eyes of their inventors — fly-fishing videotapes, Web pages, computer software, and so on— now inundate us daily. Fly fishing has been glamorized in publications ranging from *Playboy* to the *Wall Street Journal,* popularized in movies, books, and magazines aimed at the mainstream of society, and exalted in television commercials for all manner of products.

All this has profoundly affected the sociology of the sport. The most visible change, of course, is on the water, where fly fishers are much more numerous than they used to be, while fish, unfortunately, are fewer. But expansion and commercialism have brought many other changes as well, including a couple that are particularly fascinating to observers of the fly-fishing scene. One is the rise of the outdoor trade show as a marvel of marketing; the other is the growing phenomenon of the "professional" fly fisher, one who makes a full-time living from the sport. Not surprisingly, the two are closely related.

The outdoor trade show is an outrageous venture in raw capitalism. Whoever would have thought that you could get people to pay for the privilege of going shopping? For that is exactly what happens at these shows: People pay admission to buy from merchants who pay for space to display their wares. Throw in a few commercial sponsors, who pay for most of the advertising, and you have what almost amounts to a license for the show operator to print money. Whatever else you may feel about these events, you have to acknowledge the pure audacity of whoever thought up the idea.

Most of these shows are not limited exclusively to fly fishing; usually they are open to fishing of all kinds, plus hunting and other outdoor sports. But as fly fishing has grown in popularity and commercial importance, it has played an increasingly important role and now dominates many of the outdoor trade shows. In any case, the formats are all similar: row after row of display booths where manufacturers and retailers offer their products for sale, other booths with fancy lodges selling fishing or hunting trips, outdoor magazines selling subscriptions, publishers selling books, organizations selling memberships, and so on and on and on. Usually these include at least a few worthy nonprofit organizations trying to capture a small share of the public's attention, but often their booths are stuck back in the drafty corners of the hall because it costs too much for one in a prime location. Some shows exercise a minimal standard of discretion by keeping out certain types of businesses—sleazy purveyors of "vacation property" or time-share condominiums, for example—but others do not.

It's instructive just to wander around one of these shows, pushing your way through the crowded corridors between the booths, looking and listening and absorbing the curious ambience. Here you will see some of the finest products modern industrial society can offer—and some of the worst. You can inspect the very best and most expensive handmade split-bamboo fly-fishing rods or you can see rods made of cheap composites without enough guides to make a decent cast; you can find genuine works of art with an outdoor theme, or you can see gaudy pictures of bugling elk under a full moon, painted on velvet and framed in plastic. You can find the finest flies tied by the best artisans, or you can see crude lures soaked in stink bait. If you listen carefully over the great continuous waterfall sound of thousands of simultaneous conversations, you can hear duck and turkey calls, dog-training whistles, and the steady click of fly reels and credit-card machines.

As you wander up and down the aisles you can smell leather, gun oil, human sweat, and stale hot dogs. You can witness outdoor fashion statements of every kind—people wearing string ties, cowboy hats, and heavy belts fastened with bright metal buckles; others in camouflage jumpsuits with ammo belts; even a few in fancy safari jackets with Australian digger hats. Nearly every person you see will be white, the overwhelming majority will be men, and the relatively few women will mostly have bored, resigned looks on their faces.

In this vast indoor marketplace you can buy anything from packages of dyed marabou feathers to membership in a right-wing militia battalion preparing for war against the United Nations. You can shop for gun safes or finger sleeves, dog food or beef jerky, fleece-lined gloves or cheap rain gear. You can sign up for a vacation trip that will cost a third of your annual income, or decide to stay at home and invest in a backyard yurt.

Of course you don't have to buy anything. If you can resist the blandishments of the salespeople lurking in every booth, it's possible to window-shop to your heart's content, and pick up enough free brochures to fuel a whole season's worth of campfires. You can also attend lectures or demonstrations on a wide range of subjects— everything from fly casting to launching yourself in a float tube without looking ridiculous about it. You can see casters tossing lures into water tanks filled with fungus-splotched, blunt-finned old hatchery trout, or watch a video on how to gut a deer. You also have the chance to see, hear, or even obtain autographs from "celebrity speakers" (that's what the show sponsors call them), all experts of one kind or another, including fly fishers, who appear at these shows year after year. And you can do all this without spending a dime, except the price of admission.

But spending is definitely encouraged.

When these shows first started coming around I went to several of them out of curiosity, found I heartily disliked their reek of commercialism, and mostly shunned them thereafter. I also turned down invitations to be a "celebrity speaker" at several of them. But as the shows grew larger and more numerous, it became impossible to ignore the glare of publicity they generated or the obvious impact they were having on the outdoor community, and finally, as an interested observer of the sociology of fly fishing, I decided I could ignore them no longer. It was time to check them out from the inside, as a participant, to see if my private feelings of distaste were truly justified.

So the next time I was invited to be a speaker, I accepted. In fact, I did it twice. Each time I was asked to sign something called a "talent contract," and in return I was issued a pin-on badge that identified me in large bold type as a CELEBRITY SPEAKER—probably the last thing I ever wanted to be called. I felt terribly self-conscious wearing the badge—rather like a blue-ribbon cow must feel at the county fair, I suppose—but it was necessary to get past the security guard at the show gate.

I also noticed in small print on the back of the badge the schedule for a "power sales seminar." Presumably this was an event where one could pick up some pointers on how to work the crowd, and I suppose I should have attended purely for purposes of sociological research, but I couldn't quite bring myself to do so. Instead, I gave my talk before an audience that seemed only faintly interested in what I had to say; they had probably wandered into the auditorium looking for a place to sit down, since there was no place to sit outside. Afterward I sat at a table signing books and answering questions.

While I was busy doing this I accidentally overheard a conversation between a well-known "outdoor writer" and the owner of a prominent fishing lodge. They were talking loudly to make themselves heard above the constant drone of the crowd, so it was impossible not to overhear what they were saying. It soon became evident that the writer was blatantly trying to solicit a free trip from the lodge owner, and I felt embarrassed for both; the lodge owner obviously felt awkward and didn't know quite how to respond to the situation, while the famous writer kept burrowing in aggressively, promising to write a favorable story no matter how the trip turned out, prostituting himself shamelessly in the process. Later, reflecting upon what I had heard, I decided that such a conversation was nothing more than the natural consequence of the everything-has-a-price atmosphere of the outdoor show, with its constant heavy emphasis on commercialism.

The second show was much like the first, except that my stint as moderator of a panel on steelhead fly fishing was cut short by a violent earthquake, which emptied the auditorium even faster than anything I'd said. I sensed perhaps Mother Nature was trying to tell me something, and decided it was time to end my brief career as a "celebrity speaker." Besides, I had seen enough to consider that my research was complete.

Afterward, when I analyzed my feelings and impressions of these shows, I was somewhat surprised to find that they were mixed. I was still greatly bothered by the overwhelmingly pervasive atmosphere of commercialism, more than a little offended by the often unjustified glorification of so-called angling celebrities (they put their waders on one foot at a time, just like the rest of us), and upset by the memory of that ugly conversation between the outdoor writer and the lodge owner. But I had also been buoyed by the opportunity to visit many old friends and make some new ones during the two shows, and pleasantly surprised to discover that some people really do go to these events to learn something from the experts in attendance. So the shows do serve some legitimate social and educational purposes.

On the other hand, you could probably say the same thing about Wal-Mart.

As for "professional" fly fishers, I suppose there always have been a few of them, people who made their full-time living from the sport. But now there are many, and their numbers are growing rapidly. The outdoor trade show has helped make this possible by providing them with steady employment during the "show season," from November through March, when other commercial opportunities are few or nil.

These professional anglers follow a fascinating career path. Typically they start out by selling a few articles to outdoor magazines—easy enough to do, even if you can't write very well—and this gives them a little name familiarity. Then they cobble together a slide show or two and go on the lecture circuit, also easy, because every fly-fishing club is continually on the lookout for new programs and the demand for guest speakers is even greater than the demand for articles by outdoor magazines.

Exposure on the lecture circuit gives them greater name familiarity, and sooner or later this leads to other opportunities—maybe a shot as an instructor at a fly-fishing school, or a couple of guest spots on a regional outdoor television show. Maybe a book is next, then a latch-up as a "field tester" (unpaid) or later maybe even as a "consultant" (paid) for one or more tackle manufacturers. Either way, the angler gets free tackle and the manufacturer promotes his name, which makes it even more commercially valuable.

The next step, perhaps, is a listing as a "contributing editor" on the masthead of one or more of the fly-fishing magazines. This is a sweet deal because usually a "contributing editor" doesn't really have to contribute anything other than the use of his increasingly recognizable name, which, by association, the publisher hopes will boost the magazine's circulation. However, having one's name on the masthead also pretty much guarantees the magazine will buy anything the angler does happen to write, which means another ready source of income. It's also added publicity, giving the angler's name even more exposure.

After that may come more books, regular exposure as a guest or host on television shows, a prime role in one or more fly-fishing videos, the inevitable invitation to be a "celebrity speaker" on the outdoor-show circuit, endorsements of products or lodges, and the chance to "lead" groups of anglers on trips to exotic angling destinations.

These trips are an interesting social phenomenon in themselves. Sometimes they are promoted as opportunities for people to fish with angling "poets" or "legends." Those who sign up to go along are entitled to listen to any immortal pearls of wisdom that might happen to spill from the lips of the "poet," buy him extra drinks at the lodge bar, and pay for his trip as well as their own. In return, they get name-dropping rights, so later, in conversations with their fishing companions, they can say things like: "When I was with my good buddy [fill in name of 'poet'] on the Karluk," or "When [name of 'poet'] and I were fishing together in the Bahamas," and so on. For some people this seems to fill a curious psychological need, and of course for the "poet" it means free fishing trips and welcome word-of-mouth publicity.

All these activities produce income in one way or another, and all help to publicize the angler's name, which in turn leads to even further commercial opportunities in a self-perpetuating cycle. The details of each angler's ascension to the professional ranks may vary, but in general this is how it is done. Eventually the angler reaches full employment, receiving enough in cold cash or free goods to make a full-time living from the sport.

If you call that a living.

Certainly it's not about going fishing all the time. A professional fly fisher does have to work hard, doing things many people would find disagreeable. Anglers on the winter show circuit, for example, must travel to a different city each week—maybe stopping off briefly to put on a program or two for local fly-fishing clubs—and bunk in shabby motels, eat in greasy-spoon restaurants, go through the same routine time after time, recite the same tired old jokes, answer the same questions, wear the same frozen smile. It's not easy being a poet in the off season.

Yet the goal of being a full-time professional fisherman beckons more people all the time. Like big-time pro athletes, some even hire agents to search out additional commercial opportunities and make the best possible deals for them. That this is so—that it is even possible—says a lot about what has happened to fly fishing since the beginning of its commercial expansion nearly three decades ago.

What's next? Nike symbols on the sides of trout?

If you detect a note of disapproval on my part, you are perceptive. I hasten to add, however, that I am personally acquainted with many of these "professional" fly fishers, and some are among the nicest people I have ever met. I just don't happen to agree with the way they've chosen to make a living.

Wait a minute! Time out!

Who am I, you say, to disapprove of those who profit from the sport? As a writer of books and articles about fly fishing, and an editor of fly-fishing magazines, have I not profited from it myself?

The answer, of course, is yes.

Well, you say, doesn't that make me a professional fisherman too?

Hold on a minute! Let's not get carried away. It's true I have been paid for writing about fly fishing—otherwise I could never possibly justify the great expense of time and effort—but profit never has been my primary motive, and the amounts I have received probably are much smaller than you would suppose. I write about fly fishing mostly because it pleases me, because it is the best way I have of sharing the immense satisfaction I derive from the sport, and because I hope what I have to say might help others to think and feel. But I made my principal living from the newspaper business, and if I am professional at anything, it is as a writer and editor, not a fly fisher. I love the sport far too much to ever think of making it a business.

So that is my defense against the charge of professionalism. To it I would add the observation that I am as much bound by the existing system as those who have chosen to make their full-time living from fly fishing; the reality is that I cannot afford to participate in the sport in the way I have chosen without receiving some compensation. I may wish it were otherwise, but I can't escape it. And although I do not agree with those who have embraced the system to the extent of becoming full-time professional fly fishers, someone else probably would have taken advantage of the opportunity if they had not. The point is that the opportunity would not even exist had it not been for the widespread commercialization of the sport.

The evidence of that commercialization is visible in many other ways. Fly-fishing schools are one example. The first such schools were sponsored mostly by clubs or other nonprofit organizations with the unselfish motive of introducing people to the pleasures of the sport. Now most are sponsored by tackle manufacturers or local fly-fishing shops, and the underlying motives are quite different; they have less to do with creating new fly fishers than they do with creating new customers—people who will buy rods, reels, lines, flies, accessories, trips, or other goods and services. In this they have been very successful, adding considerably to the size of the fly-fishing market.

Competition for that market has caused other dramatic changes in the sport. More and more manufacturers have appeared on the scene, offering rods, reels, lines, waders, vests, clothing, accessories, and every conceivable other thing a fly fisher could want. Most extraordinary of all has been the rapid proliferation of reel manufacturers; there are now more different kinds of fly reels on the market than there are breakfast cereals. This is all to the good, for it assures consumers a greater selection than ever before.

However, another usual benefit of economic competition—lower prices—has not materialized. Instead, the opposite is true: The cost of fly fishing has gone up even faster than the rate of inflation. License fees are higher, travel costs are up, accommodations are more expensive, and more waters are coming under private management with high daily rod fees.

But these increases are nothing compared to the cost of tackle. Thirty years ago a fly fisher could purchase all the necessary tackle, plus a whole week's worth of fishing, for less than it now costs to buy a single middle-of-the-line fly reel. And that's just one example. Recently I reviewed a fishing book with a cover price of $7,500 and thumbed through a catalog of fly reels priced up to $12,000. These, thankfully, are exceptions, but they may indicate where things are going.

One reason competition has failed to drive prices down is that the fly-fishing market is finally approaching the point of saturation, forcing manufacturers to spend more heavily on advertising and promotion—including participation in trade shows, which doesn't come cheap. These added costs, which the manufacturers apparently believe are necessary to compete for or retain market share, are inevitably passed along to consumers.

Another, even more important reason for higher prices is that manufacturers charge whatever the traffic will bear—and right now the traffic is bearing a lot.

These higher costs have some potentially ominous implications for the future of the sport. They may mean that it is rapidly becoming what it has long been unjustly accused of being: a sport of the wealthy aristocracy. That stereotypical image stems from the origins of fly fishing in the British Isles, where the best fishing always has been in private hands, accessible only to the wealthy or to nobility, but until recently that has never been true in North America. Here we have a long tradition of public fishing and amateur, egalitarian participation, meaning that anyone, from any walk of life, could be a fly fisher and go fishing nearly anywhere. But the higher costs of nearly everything related to fly fishing are changing that, and now it is increasingly only the well-to-do who can afford the best tackle, the best instruction, or the best private fishing. We are meeting the enemy, and it is us.

Another inevitable consequence of higher prices will be a smaller market—the passing of the Baby Boom generation also will contribute to this—and the great commercial expansion of fly fishing will come to an end, probably with some casualties and consolidations among the tackle manufacturers. Worse yet, rising costs will limit the number of people who can afford to participate in the sport, and this in turn will erode the public support necessary to defend threatened fisheries resources. That will be especially true if minority groups, the fastest-growing segments of the population, continue their disinterest in fly fishing because they are socially and economically barred from participating in it.

There's no denying that the commercialization of fly fishing has brought many benefits—rapid technological progress, a much greater variety of products, more rapid communication and travel, easily available information and instruction, and a much higher public profile for the sport. But it has also cost the sport whatever innocence it may once have had and jeopardized its long tradition of amateur, egalitarian participation. On balance, it is difficult to say that what we have gained is worth more than what we have lost.

But the forces of change sweeping through the sport are as irresistible as the tides, and there is nothing anyone could have done to stop them. The fact is that our sport has become a business and we can only adapt to those changed circumstances and hope to make the best of it.

Or maybe I'm wrong about all this. Maybe the innocent, egalitarian days of fly fishing that I remember from my youth never really existed at all, except in my mind. Maybe fly fishing always has been a commercial sport, dominated by celebrities, and it just took a long time for that to become visible in the far-distant corner of the country where I live. Perhaps there's no harm in it anyway. Maybe I'm just hopelessly out of step.

If so, I'll probably remain that way, for I hear the cadence of my own drummer very clearly. Dame Juliana had it right when she said fly fishing is good for the soul, not for the pocketbook. I just hope the soul of fly fishing isn't up for sale.

CHAPTER FIFTEEN

Fall Guy

I followed the trail down the steep series of switchbacks into the canyon of the lower Elwha and came to the river at a great pool, a hundred yards long and a double haul wide. A heavy riffle at the head broke into strands of current that flowed through the pool from end to end, dancing and flashing in the morning sunlight. It was classic summer steelhead water.

Or so I thought, anyway. But I fished the whole length of it with a riffle-hitched dry fly and didn't raise a single fish.

What to do next? The water below looked unpromising. I thought of going through the pool a second time with a wet fly, but the prospect wasn't appealing. Once you've fished a pool, you've fished it, and it's hard to get excited about fishing it again right away. It's a little like watching recent television reruns.

I looked upstream to see if things there were any better. Above the long riffle feeding the pool I could see the dark gleam of another classic-looking pool, shaded by the canyon wall. As soon as I saw it I knew I wanted to fish it. But I could also see I would have to cross the river and fish it from the other side.

I hiked a little way upstream, looking for a place to cross, and came finally to a logjam. The weather-silvered logs were gathered in a jackstraw tangle higher than my head, so I climbed to the top and looked down at the river on the other side.

The water directly in front was at least waist deep, flowing swiftly over a rocky, irregular bottom. There was no obvious place to cross, but the water above and below looked even less promising, so if

I was to cross at all it would have to be here. Maybe once I got out into the river I could find a crossing route that wasn't obvious from my vantage point on the logjam.

That turned out to be wishful thinking. By the time I had waded to midstream the current had formed an angry curl of white water around my waist and it was all I could do to keep my balance. Things looked even worse ahead. I thought of turning back, but another glance upstream at the inviting pool changed my mind. I kept going.

Somehow—I'm still not exactly sure how—I made it without falling down or shipping water over my wader tops. Feeling very pleased with myself, I walked the rest of the way upstream to the pool.

Up close the pool was a disappointment; the tongue of white water that fed it dissolved quickly into a big back eddy that hadn't been visible from downstream. No matter where I cast, the eddy caught my fly and brought it back almost to my feet. I tried mending line to get a better drift, but it was hopeless.

Then I saw something else that hadn't been evident from downstream: The back eddy had caused an underwater gravel bar to form at the tail of the pool, extending across the river at an angle. It looked like a much easier crossing route, so I decided to follow it back to the other side of the river.

The crossing *was* easier, the bar providing a good underwater footpath until it ended at a narrow slot of deep water, which I managed to hurdle without getting wet. After that it was just a few more steps to the edge of the logjam.

I climbed again to the top and stopped to look back at the river, once more feeling highly pleased with myself for having made a safe crossing. True, I hadn't caught any steelhead, but I'd certainly waded well under difficult circumstances, and there was plenty of satisfaction in that. Probably not many fishermen had ever crossed the river at this point. Maybe I was even the first.

Feeling very smug and self-congratulatory, I turned to go.

A split second later I was hanging upside down inside the logjam. Dazed and breathless, I blinked sand out of my eyes and looked around, trying to figure out what had happened.

Somehow I'd missed a step and fallen through the top of the jam. Overhead I could see one foot wedged between a pair of logs; below, in the subdued light filtering through the jumble, I could see my glasses and fly rod on the ground, a couple of feet farther down. I was hanging by one leg, held up by the wedged foot—which suddenly began to hurt.

I tried to take stock of the situation. Only one foot was caught; the other leg and both arms were free. And although both arms were cut and bleeding, I felt no pain other than that in my foot, which was steadily getting worse.

Somehow I had to get loose, so I braced my arms against the surrounding logs and started squirming and wiggling in an effort to free my foot. It came free suddenly and I fell the rest of the way to the ground, landing heavily on one shoulder; fortunately the ground was soft and absorbed most of the impact.

It was nearly dark in the small opening at the bottom of the jam, but I could see daylight shining through openings between the logs. I crawled toward the largest opening and in a few moments emerged into warm sunshine. With a sigh of relief, I got stiffly to my feet and started checking the extent of the damage to myself and my equipment.

Other than the cuts on my arms, which weren't serious, and the painful foot, nothing seemed terribly amiss. I had recovered my glasses, my fly rod somehow had survived the fall, and—most remarkable—even my waders didn't appear to have been punctured.

But I was worried about the foot. It held when I put weight on it, so apparently it wasn't broken, but it hurt more all the time and I could feel it swelling rapidly inside my wading shoe. It probably wouldn't be up to the long, steep hike back to my car.

The best way to reduce pain and swelling is to apply ice, but of course I had none. However, there was a nice cold river close at hand. I could put my foot in that to reduce the swelling. I thought about taking everything off and soaking the foot, but it might already be so swollen I'd have trouble removing my wading shoe, so I decided just to leave the shoe on. And as long as I was going to do that—and considering that my waders weren't torn and my fly rod was still okay—I thought I might as well spend the time fishing while the cold water was soothing my swollen foot. You know, just to keep from getting bored.

So I put on a sinking line and a wet fly, limped out into the first long pool, the one I'd fished earlier, and went through it a second time. It took a full hour to cover it and in that time the cold water had the desired effect—it dulled the pain and reduced the swelling so that my foot felt a lot better. Afterward I was able to hike out of the canyon without difficulty.

It would be nice to report that I also caught a steelhead. Unfortunately, that didn't happen.

But the experience did teach me a thing or two. Thinking about what had happened—how one moment I had been feeling high and mighty about my wading prowess, and the next I was hanging upside down inside a logjam with a wedged foot and a thoroughly deflated ego—it occurred to me that fly fishing has a way of cutting people down to size whenever their heads get a little too big for their fishing hats. In fact, that may be one of the unsung virtues of the sport: As soon as we think we've mastered it, or some part of it, it shows us otherwise.

In other words, fly fishing humbles us. And that's good.

Because sometimes we have it coming.

CHAPTER SIXTEEN

The Perfect River

Some years ago I was asked to write an article describing my vision of the perfect river. As so often happens, the magazine that wanted the article was on a tight schedule and had only limited space, so I was forced to write the piece hurriedly and fill it with obvious and not very profound observations.

But that wasn't the end of the matter. For some reason the question stuck in my mind and I couldn't let go of it. What *would* the perfect river be like? Surely there would be more to it than the few hurried thoughts I'd jotted down for the magazine. So I kept thinking about it, filling in the blanks in what I had written with remembered glimpses from the rivers of several continents, mentally appending each new thought or idea, until gradually a full portrait of the perfect river began to emerge in my mind, an image I could see clearly in every detail:

The perfect river is reached by a long narrow trail through the woods, and not many people know the way. The woods are like those I remember from my youth, filled with ancient fir, spruce, and cedar, trees so tall they seem to stretch all the way up to the sky, so thick a man feels compelled to walk around their mighty trunks and look up at them with reverence and awe. Older than the nation itself, they keep the forest floor in perpetual shade, keep it carpeted in deep soft windrows of fallen needles. Moss grows along the trail, too, in layers as thick as mattresses, and the route winds back and forth through glistening hummocks of sword fern and dense salal.

It is moist here even during the hottest summer days and the brisk walk brings beads of perspiration to your brow. Here and there the soft earth holds other tracks besides your own, most made by raccoon or deer. There are only a few other human footprints, all belonging to fishermen whose names you surely know.

As you near the end of the trail you begin to hear the river even before you can see it and you recognize its voice, a hollow, deep, masculine sound that matches the river perfectly in character and strength. Its echo is an urgent summons, hurrying your footsteps.

The trail ends abruptly in a single long step down an earthen bank to a rocky bar that borders on the river. Even in your haste to reach the stream you cannot resist pausing to look at the array of rocks cluttered on the bar. There are rocks of every shape and size, every hue and color—gray and buff and brown and yellow, some with colorful ribbons of mineral running through them, others speckled with gleaming chips of mica or tiny garnets the color of blood. There are snow-white chunks of quartz, shining bits of soapstone or river jade, and crimson shards of jasper, all washed many times by the river, rinsed even more often by the rain, dried and bleached daily by the sun. Among them are just enough translucent agates that you feel lucky if you should happen to find one as you cross the bar on your way to the river.

The river itself is finally visible as a molten green-and-silver streak in the morning sunlight. On its far side the virgin forest rises in lofty ranks of dusky green, interrupted by the occasional pale scars of old lightning-caused burns. Fire-blackened spires stand forlornly in these open spaces, ragged remains of what once were mighty trees; now they are surrounded by blooming fireweed, early-turning vine maple, and the ground-hugging green-and-crimson vines of the true wild blackberry, whose tiny fruit begins to ripen just as the first bright summer steelhead start entering the river. Beyond the forest loom hazy blue mountains that hold the snow on their summits all through the long, hot summer, and here summer never ends—for how could it be otherwise on the perfect river?

At the river's edge you pause to rig up your rod and consider your prospects. Those prospects are good, for there is always a chance of hooking fish in the perfect river—and not just any fish, but the best of all fish, wild summer-run steelhead, bright and fresh from the sea. Their genes remain uncompromised by those of any hatchery fish; they are as wild and free as the river itself, their character shaped and refined by thousands of generations of evolution over the same span of time the river itself has evolved.

Still, the river also holds other fish worth catching. Bold, olive-bodied cutthroat wait in clusters behind sunken snags or under overhanging limbs, ever ready to rush a well-presented fly. Bright chinook salmon line up like metal ingots on the floors of deeper pools, and resident rainbows with rose-colored flanks rise endlessly to the river's insect hatches.

Those hatches are always abundant and visible. Caddis larvae cling to nearly every underwater rock, each tubular-shaped rocky little case an individual expression of the tiny architect within. The dried husks of hatched-out stonefly nymphs hang like ornaments from boulders exposed above the flow, and any rock turned over in the shallows will reveal a covey of mayfly nymphs nearly ready for hatching. When the hatches are under way the surface of the river is covered with flies nearly as thick as dust; rings appear everywhere, marking the quick rises of feeding fingerlings and smolts, future steelhead on the prowl.

The water in the perfect river is always cold and clear, exposing the bright rock on the river bottom—fine, rounded rock, free and clear of silt and algae so that a man can set his foot down on it firmly without fear of slipping. The wading is easy, but not too easy, just difficult enough to be challenging and sometimes exhilarating, and the current is strong enough in places to test the footing of the boldest angler.

The perfect river naturally affords the chance to hook one of its fish in the most perfect way, by having it come in a rush to a high-floating dry fly, or in a long lunge to a riffle-hitched skater slicing across the flat tailwater of a great pool. The river must have just the right kind of water for this fishing, and of course it does. It is not too large, but not too small either, its maximum width no greater than your longest double haul, its narrowest reach easily covered with a roll cast.

Besides good dry-fly water there is every other kind of water a fly fisher possibly could want. The river has many wide bends with deep runs along their outer banks where the light green water deepens into a dark, mysterious blue-green shade, frosted with flecks of foam. Between these bends are stretches of fast pocket water alternating with deeper pools filled with complex currents, and all these are connected by narrow chutes and slicks. The largest pools have long, smooth tailouts where fish rise well into the evenings.

When the sun is high enough to offer a chance of seeing well into the water, the river sometimes reveals the shadowy gray shapes of steelhead holding nervously amid the clutter of boulders on its bottom, offering the rare opportunity to stalk fish where they lie. Each pool is bordered by a long gravel bar with plenty of space free from all but the smallest fledgling willows and cottonwoods, so there is always ample room for backcasts.

One can choose to fish in solitude on the perfect river, or perhaps in the company of a single fishing partner, an old and good friend with whom all necessary words have long since been exchanged. The river also has its own cadre of resident fishermen:

the eagle, osprey, heron, and kingfisher. Along with these a day on the river usually affords the chance to see a deer wading in the shallows, or the sight of fresh bear or cougar tracks in the soft wet sand and clay along the river's shore.

The perfect river also has its own traditions. It is a river where famous anglers have fished in the past, where new methods have been tested, proven, and accepted, where useful discoveries have been made and colorful legends founded, and all these things have been recorded carefully in the pages of treasured angling books.

The river still offers the chance for an occasional meeting with one of these storied anglers, one who has made his share of discoveries and contributed his measure to its lore and traditions, someone like a Ralph Wahl or an Enos Bradner. You see him at a distance; he waves and comes forward and you exchange greetings and compare notes about the day's fishing. Then you watch while he fishes for a while and almost inevitably you learn something from the experience. Finally you wish one another well and go your separate ways.

The choice of which fly to use on the perfect river is never a matter of concern, for the best fly is always the one you happen to be using at the time. Yet there are no guarantees that even the best fly will take a steelhead, because on the perfect river, as on every river, the fish never come too easily and success is something that never can be taken for granted.

Nevertheless, there is nearly always some sort of action. Sometimes a steelhead will come short to your floating fly, rising in a great blossom of white spray that collapses on itself and disappears back into the river along with the fish. Sometimes one takes hold and lunges away on a wild run, pulling line noisily from your reel— but then the fly comes away, and you are left with only the empty feeling of the trailing line and the equally empty feeling in the pit of your stomach.

Then the next fish rises purposefully and is hooked firmly and fights like no other fish ever has. It jumps repeatedly, runs tirelessly, twists and turns and shakes itself in a wild expenditure of strength. It leaps again, high above the plane of the river, a bright silver shape suspended over a turquoise pool, a sight you will remember forever. Just as quickly it is gone again, back in the river, tearing downstream in a wild run fueled by a mixture of mortal fear and hot fury. It resists with every last ounce of its strength, every last effort of its will, and only when both you and the fish are nearly exhausted is it finally possible to lead it to the beach.

Like most fish in the perfect river it is not of record size; the steelhead here are large and strong enough to show what they can do, and that is as large and strong as they need to be. Yet occasionally the river yields a steelhead bigger than nearly all the rest, a great wise old fish that is a veteran of several spawning runs, one that has spent more time at sea and in the river than any of its fellows, and some-how—by virtue of greater strength, stouter heart, or superior will—attained a size large enough to take your breath away.

Your first thought is for the strength of the slender tippet that connects you with the fish. Sometimes the tippet holds and some-times it does not, for even on the perfect river not every fish is brought to hand. But if it does hold, if all goes well, if after a long fight the fish is finally landed, then it is always mint bright, clean and perfect, graceful and wild, and certainly worth a few moments' admiration before you remove the hook and slip it back into the emerald currents from which it came. For that is the best fate for any fish taken fairly on the fly, and returning it helps assure the future of the run—no less important in the perfect river than any other.

Somewhere along the banks of the perfect river is a place where rocks have been gathered in a circle to hold a driftwood campfire, and that is where you go at the end of the day. Your fishing partner is there already and has the fire going, and the two of you crouch next to it, staring into its livid coals, inhaling the tang of its smoldering driftwood, sipping coffee perhaps laced with a little whiskey, and talk of the day's fishing. As always, the enjoyment of the day is enhanced by sharing the experience with a friend.

Finally, when it is time to go, you scatter the ashes from the fire and cover them with coarse sand carried down from the hills by the river. Then you start back along the familiar trail, now barely visible in the long light of a summer evening, and stop briefly for a last look back at the river. Bats are busy making their silent strafing runs through the evening hatch, and off in the dark woods you can hear the owls waking. The river's soft, deep voice follows you far up the trail, fading at last to a hollow whisper until you are no longer certain whether it is the river or your own imagination that you hear.

And that is my vision of the perfect river.

You may think it is only a fantasy, a bold dream, or perhaps just a wild flight of imagination, because logic dictates nothing of the kind could ever truly exist.

Yet it does.

The perfect river flows ever through my consciousness, a composite of the best features of all the rivers I have ever fished, a blend of fond memories of big fish and old friends, of dear places far and near. It is always there, ever murmuring in the background of my mind, ever waiting to be fished, always generous, never disappointing. I have only to close my eyes for a moment to see again its bright silver gleam, to watch my fly settle once more on its crystalline currents, to see the rise that will surely follow.

It is my river and forever shall be, and I keep it well stocked with memories, hopes, and dreams. It courses swiftly through my veins, hurrying always toward its destiny. It is the river of my heart.